And Thereby Hangs A Tale

DAVID TEEMS

HARVEST HOUSE PUBLISHERS

EUGENE, OREGON

Published in association with Rosenbaum & Associates Literary Agency, Inc., Brentwood, Ten-nessee.

Cover photo © iStockphoto / InkkStudios

Cover design by Left Coast Design, Portland, Oregon

AND THEREBY HANGS A TALE
Copyright © 2010 by David Teems
Published by Harvest House Publishers
Eugene, Oregon 97402
www.harvesthousepublishers.com

Library of Congress Cataloging-in-Publication Data
Teems, David.
And thereby hangs a tale / David Teems.
    p. cm.
Includes bibliographical references.
ISBN 978-0-7369-2716-1 (pbk.)
1. Dog owners—Religious life. 2. Dogs—Religious aspects—Christianity. I. Title.
BV4596.A54T44 2010
248.4—dc22
                                                                    2009044013

Printed in the United States of America

10 11 12 13 14 15 16 17 18 / BP-SK / 10 9 8 7 6 5 4 3 2 1

To the three of them.
They know who they are.
They always did.

And to Huckleberry Hound, the
only blue dog I ever knew.

acknowledgments

My indebtedness is rather exhaustive, but so is my gratitude.

- To Randy Elliott, for his optimism, for his immutable friendship, and, in an indirect sense, for setting this book in motion.

- To Ann Elliott, not the character in Jane Austen's book, but Randy's wife, the first to read these pages, who came up smiling and wanted to go buy a dog.

- To Bucky Rosenbaum, the Author Whisperer, my agent and friend.

- To Carol Kelly, my editorial fairy godmother.

- To Matt and Julie Kelly, for simply being Matt and Julie Kelly.

- To my sons, Adam and Shad, who were there, who make this little history even richer.

- To our Katie, Julian, Evie, and Audrey Gray.

- To my mother.

- And to Benita, always. Always.

contents

Now ask the beasts, and they will teach you;
and the birds of the air, and they will tell you;
or speak to the earth, and it will teach you;
and the fish of the sea will explain to you.

JOB 12:7-8 NKJV

an uncommon love

IT IS SOMETHING YOU MIGHT SAY when meaning is implied but not stated, when there is more to be said than is actually spoken. The artful gossip might employ it as a tease. When William Shakespeare minted the phrase "and thereby hangs a tale," the context was playful and not without his usual mischief. It was a title I could hardly resist, considering my hosts.

I am not sure I have enjoyed working on anything as much in my life as I have this present book. I can only hope that is reflected in the reading. The long hours, the retracing of memories—some of them sad, all of them fond—the migration this book made from obscurity to print, the pilgrimage it made in my own heart, my love-afflicted fascination with these amazing creatures who brought something to our young household I may never totally understand or appreciate— all these things made the completion of the task somewhat difficult. I just didn't want it to end.

This book is part tribute, part confession, part requiem for three beloved and irreplaceable friends. It may even be part Sunday school lesson, though the last thing I wanted to do was to preach or teach. It is a matter of tone I think, and anyway, the more I thought about it, the more I realized just how good our dogs were for a useful and delightful metaphor to say a few things about *the devoted life,* which is simply a way of saying that worship, far from being an isolated event, is a way of life, a continuous living current between my master and me.

It rises with me at dawn. It follows me about during the day, instructing, comforting, correcting, encouraging. And it never stops.

The devoted life is a life of uncommon love. I would say *unconditional* love, but I would then have to ask, "Is there any other kind?" I don't mean to sound glib, but when it comes to the realization of such a life, it truly is all or nothing. A plunge. A submersion. A love that saturates the whole of life to the smallest particulars. The cup of coffee with a friend, the small miracle of conversation, even the afternoon nap are sweetened with as much of the life of God as the prayer I make at the altar. Life and faith become indistinguishable.

As you read, you may think that our dogs were charmed or that I am making stuff up, fabricating, inventing. Perhaps they did live charmed lives—all three of them. If so, devotion was their coin of purchase. But I have remained as true as I know how to the memory of those days. That is the real miracle of it—I have not made anything up. Where I botched a story here or there or where I got my dates wrong, my wife has been kind enough to correct me.

Of course, the devoted life is much easier to talk about than it is to actually live, and to find a suitable model was not that easy. A friend of mine actually suggested horses, but there were at least two reasons why that wouldn't work. One, I have never had a horse. As great an animal as I know them to be, as dedicated as I understand they are to man, I have no personal experience with them, at least not enough to create a convincing metaphor.

The second reason is the easiest. A horse can't jump in your lap. It can't sleep on your bed or by your desk, and they take up way too much room. It is difficult to pretend they are not there. Plus my wife goes into a mild state of euphoria at the very mention of a horse, and the idea is to gain your attention, not to lose it to a fantasy.

I am more familiar with the emotional indicators of a dog. A horse doesn't wag its tail when it is happy, it doesn't turn around three times before lying down, and I have never seen a horse with its head out the window of a car.

So dog is it.

It was my agent who suggested horses, but with a name like Bucky what can you expect?

Enjoy yourself. You hold in your hands a small, compact world to be explored in what portions you choose, big or small. The great risk is self-examination. And perhaps rediscovery.

Keep the heart available. I am not sure there are any other rules.

David Teems

1

so inevitably dog

THERE WAS REAL MEDICINE IN THEM, and not only were they generous in the distribution of this medicine, they provided the sugar to help it go down. Love was easy. It had no conditions. It was untamed and uncivilized, as love should be. It was immediate and relevant, and it had no agenda but itself. And they never seemed to tire of it; time itself being the nonissue it was to them.

They took panic and severity from our lives and gave us back animation and color. They extended our playtime. They took the dullness out of things. They imposed their good sense of citizenship and bounce upon us, adding a buoyancy to our lives, elasticity and stretch. They taught us how to bound and bolt from our enclosures. They taught us to be curious, to be explorers, pioneers. They taught us not to care too much what others thought. Always tugging at the kid in me, they kept something young in our house.

They taught us the importance of a good nap and having a warm place in the sun. They taught us the importance of a good nose and to stretch first thing in the morning. There was no guesswork about their devotion, and it was easy to be devoted to them in return. Something mutual grew between us—naturally, casually, and in daily installments. They suited our personalities, our temperaments, our own private need for belonging. They filled out our little circle of warmth. The dogs were an intimate part of us, and we grew together.

They taught us what little work devotion can be; that innocence lives by a faith it little thinks of and that needs little labor, if any, to sustain it. They showed us that nature in us *can* be redeemed and retrained; that unlearning, though difficult, may be necessary; that old dogs *can* be taught new tricks.

They have no plans to worry them. Everything is *now*. If you don't believe that, watch them eat. Immediacy is all.

Dogs have an indifference to wealth that is difficult to understand, as well as an indifference to trends and fashions of the hour. Celebrity means nothing to them. They are unmoved by the media.

> Love was easy. It had no conditions. It was untamed and uncivilized, as love should be. It was immediate and relevant, and it had no agenda but itself.

They seem to live life authentically, in every moment, which is itself a form of worship, that is, living according to an original design and to the delight of the Creator of that design. A dog knows no other option, having no thought of or any real concept of tomorrow, taking life in with the wolfish gulp.

Outside of an occasional howl, whine, or whimper, a bark, growl, or pant, even the love croon, they had no audible language and therefore they had to *show* me their devotion outside of words, by the simple art of being themselves. They had to give devotion a shape that was louder, deeper, and truer than tongues.

Love was animated. It was conspicuous, playful, kind, without pretense. They could not hide what they felt. They saw little point in it. They were neither political nor guarded. They could not wrap themselves in protective coverings. They had not learned from us the art of disguising or suppressing what they felt. They were who they were. They accepted the mystery of me, the *other* I seemed to be to them. They didn't know how to question it, so they didn't bother.

Devotion for them was a way of life. And they made it look easy. I envied them, and yet the mirror they held up seemed to suggest possibilities—bright and hopeful possibilities that I might discover something similar about my own nature. That I too might live authentically, that I might live life as it was designed to be lived—at capacity, at full measures, and with fewer restraints. All this, and with love at the very heart of it, a love that becomes the undersong of life, as natural as breathing.

* *

For dogs, loyalty is the desire to be together with the loved one, to be where one belongs.

JEFFREY MASSON
A DOG NEVER LIES ABOUT LOVE

* *

I prithee, sweet wag!

The homage we pay to the dog is nothing new. She has maintained a presence in literature consistently since man was first able to record his thoughts. I suspect that an image of the dog—or something like the dog—was painted on cave walls. It seems we can't get enough of them, these creatures that are so purely themselves and that love with such genuine effervescence.

The following passage was written not about a man or a woman in love, nor was it written about the mechanism of worship in the human heart, in spite of how precise an image it makes. It was written about a dog:

> [Love] manifested itself to him as a void in his being—a hungry, aching, yearning void that clamored to be filled. It was a pain and an unrest; and it received easement only by the touch of the new god's presence. At such times love was joy to him, a wild, keen-thrilling satisfaction. But when away from his god, the pain and the unrest returned; the void in

him sprang up and pressed against him with its emptiness,
and the hunger gnawed and gnawed unceasingly.

—JACK LONDON, *WHITE FANG*

This is not just another portrait of warmth and loyalty. The devoted
life will ask much more than that. The springs of life are deep, and
for too many of us, untouched. Life by toleration, not by enjoyment.
Unaware there is anything more, we too often limit ourselves to the
shallows and deny what is so very close to us—that which is perhaps
one surrender, one small death beyond our reach.

Genuine love is severe. It is costly, the way as treacherous as it is narrow and steep. But we are not left to our own devices. Not trusting us
to figure love out for ourselves, Christ showed us how it is to be done.
Having botched it so completely as we are given to do, he showed us
what love looks like, how it behaves, the submission it demands, the
surrender it cannot do without. He came that we might see the divine
within each of us; that we might know what authenticity means. At the
cost of his own life, he bought back heaven for us, and with it bought
back our truest humanity. There is no better image of love.

Outside of that, nature has given us the dog.

In the entire animal kingdom, the dog is the only creature who
has dared to cross the threshold that separates her from a being totally
unlike herself, the only creature that has made successful pilgrimage from one realm to another. Desire outweighed consequence. By
some irrepressible magnetism, the dog alone overcame the obstacles,
crossed the divide, and made herself a home there. And she did it for
one reason: to be close to man. He was god, after all. Or at least the
dog was convinced he was.

> Man loves the dog, but how much more ought he to love
> it if he considered, in the inflexible harmony of the laws of
> nature, the sole exception, which is that love of a being that
> succeeds in piercing, in order to draw closer to us, the par-
> titions, every elsewhere impermeable, that separate the spe-
> cies!…Amid all the forms of life that surround us, not one,
> excepting the dog, has made an alliance with us.
>
> One animal alone, among all that breathes upon the earth, has

succeeded in breaking through the prophetic circle, in escaping from itself to come bounding toward us, definitely to cross the enormous zone of darkness, ice and silence that isolates each category of existence in nature's unintelligible plan.

—MAURICE MAETERLINCK, *OUR FRIEND THE DOG*

The devoted life is a pilgrimage, an incredible journey across a divide, across an "enormous zone of darkness, ice and silence." I struggle against the elements that I might be close to him I love, that I might inhabit his world, that I might make a home there.

· ·

The only one who can teach me to find
God is God, Himself, Alone.

THOMAS MERTON
NEW SEEDS OF CONTEMPLATION

· ·

beyond human likeness

Obviously, we are working within a playful, but nonetheless powerful metaphor, and the most effective metaphor, like music or perfume, works best by suggestion, not overthrow. Maybe the best way to learn is not to know we're being taught, where there are no exams, no monitors, no grades to worry us. Lessons learned in the simple and not-so-simple habit of living, the incidental kind, learned in love, love that has the naked power to bring out the tender and the best in each of us; love that asks something authentic from us; love that is not afraid to come out and play, to rally the child again; love that could be trusted because of an ancient fidelity in their animal blood, by an intelligence that grew between us, a faithfulness set like a law within them, the first commandment fixed in them like a code of life. When I dared to think the same conditions could exist between God and me, I understood their contentment.

Each of our dogs was unique. Each had their own distinct personality, their own separate set of demands, their own peculiar strengths, requirements, and preferences. Each had their own measure of neediness and complications, their own peculiar arrangement of spots. In those things, they were pretty much like the rest of us. They were not perfect, any more than you and I are perfect. And long after this metaphor has spun itself out, we will still be talking about dogs, dogs that, at times, do disgusting dog things. Nonetheless, each of them possessed an enviable spirit.

In the beginning we had one dog—a Dalmatian. We named her Oreo. She was a great dog, and that was the problem. After three or so years of her, we wanted more. We wanted a whole houseful of what she gave to us. Love with that much bounce is rare indeed. In time, we bred her with a distant cousin, a prizewinner named London. We kept two of the ten puppies that followed—one male and one female we named Salem and Savannah.

After all the cuteness wore off, and as they grew, we quickly learned that three is not one. Something changed. They became more recognizably animal, less like us. There were different rules—rules we all had to learn and accept, different dynamics, pack laws, tribal imperatives that were not present with just one dog.

> The springs of life are deep, and for too many of us, untouched.

One dog alone is fairly civilized, tranquil. Three is a sitcom. Oreo, who had shown profound devotion and attachment, what might easily be called *worship* when she was the only dog, was now competing for place. Her psychology seemed to change. We could sense her frustration in the shuffle. It was easy to feel we had lost something of her in the addition of the other two, but these were only appearances. Truth is, she had love enough to meet the needs of her new role as pack matriarch and that of loving devotee.

Even so, my wife, Benita, and I could tell Oreo grieved the slight distance between us that motherhood seemed to impose on her. But with nature duly aroused, she was a good mom: an attentive, patient mom who lived according to script, especially in the early weeks of motherhood when she was host to a sort of king-of-the-mountain, eight-is-not-enough kind of puppy brawl. Still, her eyes gave her away.

"I want to be with you," they said, *"but at the moment I'm providing dinner for ten."*

Does that rob us of our metaphor? Not in the least. Something was enhanced by the change. Community was engaged.

Though their first devotion was to us, the dogs were devoted to each other as well. They almost seemed to mimic us. Of course, I never scrapped with my sons or my wife over a bowl of food or a place to sleep, and we only occasionally hoarded our toys. But beyond that, the dogs got their cues from us. All three of them were warm, protective, and generous in their love. They were trusting, gentle, and uncommonly devoted—things that could be said of any one of us in our household. Although I didn't think about it at the time, they demonstrated another powerful element of the devoted life: *identification with the master.* We mimic what we love.

With all the changes, with all the upheaval and revolution in our little country of seven, devotion remained the first order among all of us. Oreo seemed to favor our son Shad. He was four. Maybe it was her awakened maternity that made her protective over the smallest of us. Maybe it was his height, so much closer to her own. Salem had this crush on Benita that was obvious. To Savannah, I was god.

Adam, our oldest son, who was 11 at the time, was a source of fascination to them. His youth, his own alpha standing with his brother, his assertiveness, his own bounce, even his aloofness; these things endeared him to all three of the dogs. It was a real treat for Adam to give them attention.

Their devotion was truly beyond human likeness, and their method of teaching me was so subtle that in the mutual adoration that grew and prospered among us I was not aware that *I* had become the student in this school of love.

* * * * * * * * * * * * * * * * * * * *

Dogs register no need to theorize about love (or about anything else for that matter), they just show it.

JEFFREY MASSON
DOGS NEVER LIE ABOUT LOVE

* * * * * * * * * * * * * * * * * * * *

our little plot of eden

As sweet and as memorable as those times were, they couldn't last. The canine life span is regrettably brief. Time and inevitability eventually caught up with our little plot of Eden. Life sped by us, as it does, and in its wake left only one dog: Savannah. After 12 years with the three of them, it came down to her.

It was a crisp December afternoon. There were no clouds in the sky, and other than a slight chill, sorrow seemed to have no place in such a day. They went together. Oreo and Salem had developed an observable attachment to each other over the years, so this was the only justice we could find in the whole messy thing.

Christmas was one week away. My father had died less than a year before. The wound was still raw and unsettled, and whatever grief I had suppressed, evaded, denied, buried, or sublimated for my dad got flushed to the surface again, and in full measure. It came back to me clearly, uninvited and undiminished, the ghost of Christmas past, as if it wasn't finished with me. It was relentless. I was a child again. I was blind with grief. The pain was like nothing I had felt before.

These dogs lived and moved in our intimate circle. They were a part of us. Oreo had been the pioneer who brought us to the new world. They had summoned the boy in me and allowed me to know him again, to retrace my steps. They taught my boys how to care, how to lead, how to accept love, and how to exchange it without conditions and without reserve. They taught us all lessons of belongingness.

> Love is the highest praise we may offer to God.

I felt guilty for having to make the awful decision concerning two sick dogs. I felt guilty as well for putting that decision off again and again, making the two of them suffer one more day, hoping Oreo might go quietly in her sleep or that Salem's arthritis might respond to my prayers, that we might not hear him cry in the night. I had not realized until those approaching moments just how attached I was to them, just how deep the investments were among all of us.

Recovery took days, but when I surfaced at last, Savannah was my one solace. She was now alone and had free rein in our world.

But it wasn't the adjustment you might think. Even when the three of them were together, she was separate somehow, excluded in a dog sort of way.

Savannah had one attachment. It was animal clear, and she made it obvious to all of us, including the other two dogs. She had one love, one true master, one deity of sorts, and it happened to be me. Understanding nothing of English outside of a few commands, which she hardly obeyed anyway, she nonetheless provided the metaphor that drives this little book. Though Oreo and Salem will make appearances again and again, the remainder of this tale is all hers.

The change was abrupt, the void conspicuous. Savannah grieved in her own private dog way. We knew that. But whatever heaviness, whatever her state of mind, it didn't take much time at all after that bitter December for Savannah to adjust to her new status as family dog. There was suddenly no competition for food, water, toys, attention, or anything else. She liked the new arrangement. And she had me all to herself. We detected a kind of bewilderment at first, a slip of suspicion as mild as it was fleeting, a good head-tilting, ear-raising, this-is-too-good-to-be-true kind of misgiving. As if the other two had died, and she went to heaven.

Their sermons were not loud, but they were effective. In time we heard every one of them. It is my hope that you will too, that they might encourage the lover in each of us, the lover that is synonymous with the name "Christian"; that you and I might live according to our original blueprint; that we might love without condition or impediment, for *love is the highest praise we may offer unto God,* love that mirrors him who is love.[1] That we might know the hunger that searches for him at daybreak, that determines the course of all our waking hours, right down to the God-winning moments, until we make our little circles, flop down to bed, and draw the last long sigh of night.

a work of rediscovery

The great suggestion here is that the devoted life is not only possible, but that it may be more natural to us than we first suspected. Christianity is about so many things. Maybe too many things. We make faith too much work, more than it has to be. We have given it too many names and raised too many arguments. We have lost that sense of desperation that gave Christianity a beginning. Our dependence has lost the immediacy and the depth it once had. We have exchanged human warmth and connectivity for religion, reducing much of it to the maintenance of an argument or an agenda. The devoted life can give us redemption from these things.

Dogs may typically outlove us; they may be more conspicuous and more liberal in their demonstration of that love; their company might even be preferred over yours or mine at times, but there is at least one thing that can never be said of them. You and I are endowed with something far beyond them, something that separates us from all creation. *You and I are made in the image of God.* We reflect him. We mirror him like no other creature. And God is love. Therefore, *not* to love, *not* to live the devoted life, the surrendered life, is *not* to reflect that image, is *not* to be like him, is *not* to live according to our deeper nature, is *not* to be our true selves at all.

* * * * * * * * * * * * * * * * * * * *

To say that I am made in the image of God is to say that love is the reason for my existence, for God is love. Love is my true identity. Selflessness is my true self. Love is my true character.

THOMAS MERTON
NEW SEEDS OF CONTEMPLATION

* * * * * * * * * * * * * * * * * * * *

There is a work of rediscovery before us. It will involve learning and unlearning, doing and undoing. It will mean unraveling the tight weave of habit and all binding threads, all the fictions of our lives, the many household myths that war against the heart and distance us from our God. This is as true for our private household as it is for the household of faith.

It will mean asking reason to step down from its high place. It will mean responding to love's least request of us, perhaps another death inward, another selfless act, small or large, hidden or public. It will mean we become yielding, pliant, that we become lower main- tenance, that we might find new measures of trust and surrender within, things understood only in love. That we might find honor in tenderness again, in meekness, in selflessness so contrary to the age and to the high church of man. That we might rediscover the authority in gentleness again, the sovereignty in a single act of kindness. That we might sit at the master's feet for hours, asking nothing, making no prayer but life itself.

Finally, in spite of the fun I'm having with this and the fun I hope you will have in the coming pages, I know dogs well enough not to speak too anthropomorphically of them, to make them look and act too much like you and me, to append too much of our own shapes and characteristics to them. The metaphor will stretch only as much as it needs to. And besides, to make them appear too human, well, that would be unfair to the dogs.

• • • • • • • • • • as we embark • • • • • • • • • • • •

I want to live the devoted life, to live life according to your original design, Lord. I am a world whose true discovery is yet to be. Call forth what is authentic in me, what may have been lost in my distractions, set aside, or forgotten. Set worship adrift in me. Awaken my heart, the Eden sleeping in me. I submit to all my teachers, to those you have set before, around, and above me, seen and unseen, including those I may have ignored or overlooked. I submit to the wonders of creation—to the earth and skies, to the rush and shuffle of day, and to the dark catechesis of night. Let none be silent on my behalf. I will listen for instruction. I will suffer their gentle rebuke that I may find the rule of life, that I may discover my authentic self and possess the very knowledge I sought for so long in my misbelief. Let worship flourish; let it prosper in me. Let it filter into the very lengths and limits of me, into the full sum of who I am. I will soften under your teaching.

In Christ, all that love has to say to me. Amen.

May love give you access to the higher instincts within you,
those we share with divinity,
that we may have lost in our distractions
or in our attempts to explain.

2

presence is everything

You have made known to me the path of life;
you will fill me with joy in your presence,
with eternal pleasures at your right hand.

PSALM 16:11

How gently and lovingly thou awakenest in my bosom,
Where thou dwellest secretly and alone!
And in thy sweet breathing, full of blessing and glory,
How delicately thou inspirest my love!

ST. JOHN OF THE CROSS
LIVING FLAME OF LOVE

SHE COULD SIT AT MY FEET FOR HOURS and ask nothing of me. *Being there* was all that mattered. This was true whether I even acknowledged her or paid any attention to her. She had one purpose in life, and that was to be near me. Again, being there, being allowed to sit quietly and unnoticed at my feet, or at least close by, was about as good as life got. Her contentment needed little else to be satisfied. *Presence was everything.* It was sufficient. And, no, I am not talking about my wife. I am referring to our dog Savannah.

Happy riot broke out when I returned from a trip. Whether I was gone five minutes or five days, it didn't matter. I was back. I was with them again. They would go at it with all their might and with hosannas of pure dog joy. The bright panic of love would last until something settled among them all.

The *immediacy of presence*, of my presence, of their master being there in the midst of them, approachable, touchable, attending them, accepting their homage, calmed something in them as sure and as complete as the fuss it made in the first place. Praise and pleasure melted one into the other so naturally, so completely and sufficiently, as to restore Eden in the midst of us. Eden (עֵדֶן *ay'-den*) means "pleasure."

> They would go at it with all their might and with hosannas of pure dog joy.

With three dogs, riot was a fairly common way of showing affection, and there was little we could do to stop it, even if we had wanted to. When Savannah was alone and there were no other dogs to aggravate her energies, she would go through the entire ritual of hello all by herself. King David on the streets of the great city, dancing. Even at the end, when her legs began to stiffen with age, she did her best to come to me. *Shuffle, skip, shuffle, shuffle, pause...shuffle some more.*

Most of the time when she began this sequence, I would go to her. But whatever she had to do, she would do. The desire to be close to me was much greater than the pain it took to achieve it. Desire outweighed consequence. She never complained. And the calm that followed was as alive with joy as the riot that preceded it. Contentment settling into our reserves, renewing, refreshing.

I enjoyed the "highness" I had among our dogs and the veneration that accompanied it. It gave me something to look forward to, an anticipation that was fun. Coming home was never without celebration. Love was immediate and unsophisticated. I envied this about them. And they never tired of it. We were all a part of it. They would have it no other way.

Their alarms were set off easily—the tone of my voice, the shuffle of feet they recognized as mine, the sound of a car in the driveway. It didn't take much to set love off, that beautifully wild pant and clamor of dog love.

- -

*Love for God is ecstatic, making us go out from
ourselves: it does not allow the lover to belong any
more to himself, but he belongs only to the Beloved.*

SAINT DIONYSIUS THE AREOPAGITE

- -

Their world was small, but it was a world of contentment—of warmth, belongingness, and nurture, into which each of our dogs contributed his or her part. We all made the necessary investments, and we all drew from the same household account. As dominant as we were among them, love was never one-sided. It was always mutual, and it never aged.

Assimilation into our spaces came natural to them. It seemed to take as little effort as anything else. They understood, and quickly, how and where everyone fit: who was head, who was not, how I felt toward Benita and the boys, how the boys felt about each other.

They studied us. They always studied us. They were always close enough, engaged enough, and vigilant enough to understand the subtleties of each of us. Each movement was full of meaning. They seemed to know when we needed to be left alone and when it was time to play.

> It didn't take much to set love off, that beautifully wild pant and clamor of dog love.

They anticipated our moves. They seemed to have a sense of when we were approachable, when we were game, and when we were not. They judged by the power of our distractions: how engaged we might seem on the phone, the modulations in our voices, the severity on our faces, the wrinkles on our foreheads, the way we walked about the house at any given time—the gait, the pace.

The dogs understood our affections, how we administered them, how we withheld them, and so on. They had a nose for these things, an evolved social sense. And who knows? Certain emotional states may even come with a smell. I know I have had my own suspicions.

They knew me well. They tread a world that had my signature upon it, and they were ever about the business of making peace with that world. Salem was always trying to impress Benita. She was his contentment. She brought out the low contented animal groan in him. (She has the same effect on me, but that's for another book.)

grasp of the authentic

Whoever we loved, they loved. Truth is, they tended to love everybody and saw little need in consulting us. Everybody was a potential friend. But there were exceptions.

Years ago a certain man became friends with Benita and me: a Christian man, a seemingly honorable man, a man whose sincerity seemed unquestioned, who prayed with us many times, and even wept on occasion. We treated him as we did all our friends, with acceptance and trust. He was a few years older than me, so our relationship had sort of an elder brother element to it. We confided in him with little reserve.

> Unlike us, duplicity is not something a dog understands or has to suffer from another dog. It is a uniquely human convention. The dog wouldn't see much point in it.

The dogs had a different opinion.

In spite of all the pleasantries and all the appearances of good will, they were suspicious from the beginning, from the first time the man entered our house. Before he ever opened his mouth, they were circumspect. He tried to gain their trust and friendship, but it never took. They were skittish around him, timid, tetchy. They would tiptoe out of the room if he appeared. Savannah growled at him once. Salem would crawl under our bed.

Benita and I could never quite figure the whole thing out. We laughed with the man and wrote it off to something quirky in the dogs. Their behavior toward him was consistent. Whenever he came to our house, you could see the change come over them—the wariness, the caution.

> Their power of discernment became a source of wonder and speculation. After all, we were supposed to be the higher life form.

Anyway, after some time, the man turned on my wife and me, and in our own home. It was ugly, and it was unforeseen. We didn't see it coming from any direction. The dogs did. Their vision was clear. Their grasp of the authentic was much more defined than ours. Unlike us, duplicity is not something a dog understands or has to suffer from another dog. It is a uniquely human convention. The dog wouldn't see much point in it.

They didn't gloat or say, "I told you so." They wouldn't see much point in that either. Detecting something fallen about Benita and me, they did their best to comfort us. They were good at that. It seemed a specialty of theirs. "Is it okay if I just sit here with you?" It was medicine enough.

Their power of discernment became a source of wonder and speculation. After all, we were supposed to be the higher life form. How could they judge so accurately? How could their assessments be so precise when ours were so lopsided? I don't have a satisfying answer, but I can suggest two possibilities, both essential elements of the devoted life.

By spending time with us, by observing our habits, down to the particulars, by an intense animal vigilance, they gained an intimate knowledge of us. The more they were with us, the more they wanted to be with us. There was no surfeit or saturation. There was no wearing out of their attachment. They were jealous for the privilege of being with us. It gave meaning to life.

They not only learned us with precision, they learned what was *not* us. They had an understanding of contrary spirits, those individuals who were *not* like their master or anyone of his household. Their understanding was not clouded by the usual deceptions that burden the rest of us. It was easy for them to navigate their world. The waters were clear. Their faith was simple. They lived in the confidence of the love we gave them. We, however, were distracted, led by appearances. Our vision was cluttered. Among so many things, I began to envy them that gift as well.

But there is something else. Dogs are utterly themselves. They are utterly genuine. And perhaps this authenticity allows them to sense what is authentic. It is only a suggestion, but perhaps it is just that simple. The ability to discern the truth, truth stripped of all excess, is a great advantage in the wild.

* * * * * * * * * * * * * * * * * * * *

Dear friends, do not believe every spirit.

1 JOHN 4:1

* * * * * * * * * * * * * * * * * * * *

This authenticity is perhaps the greatest benefit of the devoted life. I can be ultimately who I am, who God created me to be by peculiar design, beyond artifice, beyond the myths and counterfeits.

In living genuinely, I am able to *see* genuinely. I can live intimately with the truth of my existence because love clarifies me, it strips me of all idols, all images that are contrary to the truth, contrary to that which is authentic. In living intimately with the truth of my own existence, I am able to live intimately with all truth.[1] I am able to tell the genuine from the mirage.

I think that was their secret. In the man who was our friend who proved not to be so friendly, we saw one thing; the dogs saw something altogether different. I wish I had been paying more attention. Of course, I am speaking again in metaphor. They are just dogs, after all. Maybe, as the devoted tend to do, they just wanted to find me in everything, and with certain folks there was nothing there, no reference, no reflection of their master at all.

it all resembled faith

My closet was a place to nap in my absence, a place to pout or sulk. It offered sanctuary, refuge against the small anguish of separation. Any place I left my prints, anywhere my shadow lingered or my scent— the paths I walked, the chairs I sat in, the hallways, the rooms—as long as there was something of me in these places, the dogs could find some measure of contentment until my return. Beyond our little realm, or too far beyond those things associated with my presence, contentment was more elusive. Each morning began with a search for me, or so I was told.

I was more to them than the mere alpha of our little pack.[2] I was master. And once decided, they never questioned it. I was *other*, higher, the one to whom their worship, their loyalty, and their submission was due. Though Benita took the honors when I was not around, to them I was still *it*. One author put it this way:

> It is a deep-lying patriarchal instinct in the dog which leads
> him to recognize and honour in the man of the house and
> head of the family his absolute master and overlord, protector

of the hearth, and to find in the relation of vassalage to him
the basis and value of his own existence.

—THOMAS MANN, *"A MAN AND HIS DOG," DEATH IN VENICE*

I was sovereign over their world. Whether they saw me as another dog,
I don't know. Whether I subconsciously attributed a certain humanity
to them, that is not impossible either. But somewhere in the middle of
our perceptions of each other, we became attached. Though the devotion was mutual, I never lost headship. They treated me accordingly.
They were submissive to the hierarchy that existed in our home, the
social architecture that determined position and rank, as if they were
sure how it all worked. They did it better than we did.

Trust was easy for them. They had grown up with it, and it never
failed them. We were a mystery to them, as objects of worship usually are, but they were not afraid. What uncertainty there was only
made certainty that much sweeter. It all resembled faith. We seemed
to trigger all the finer instincts of their devotion.

Aside from my role as "deity," I was also playtime. I was recess. I
was the maypole. I was the drowse of sleep at midday. I was the lazy
stroll deep in the afternoon. I was the sit-around-and-do-nothing-if-
you-choose-I-don't-care-I-just-like-being-with-you guy.

But let's be fair. You and I live in a bigger world. Bigger demands
are made of us. What responsibilities can dogs possibly have? Their
stresses and anxieties are of a different pitch than ours. They have one
voice to answer to. You and I have many. We seem to be fascinated
by our distractions. They are unbothered by them. We do not allow
ourselves to live in a perpetual *now,* even if we understood what that
meant. We bind ourselves submissively to the clock and see no virtue
in spending long idling time doing nothing. Because we are creatures
of community, we hesitate to take life in by that same wolfish gulp.
We play nice. We are civilized. We do not scratch in public. We do
not relieve ourselves in the yard. With maybe a few exceptions, we
do not chase our tails.

Sure, dogs are better at devotion than we are. How could they not
be? Life is simpler. Faith and belief are simpler. The dog enjoys a less
complicated psychology.

* * * * * * * * * * * * * * * * * * *

The load they bear is lighter,
Than the one we bear, it's true.
They have four legs to carry theirs;
We have only two.

* * * * * * * * * * * * * * * * * * *

My dogs did not concern themselves with career maneuvering or the fulfillment of a dream. For them, life was immediate. It was fully present, something to be lived, not merely longed for. Life was something they got more out of and in less time. Other than the effort it took to seek me out, to find food when hungry, or to find a soft spot to lie down, my dogs did not strive at all.

They knew they were cared for. They had a deep animal confidence in their own devotion and in ours. It was not an issue of concern with them. They knew both to be stable and immovable. Sustenance, nurture, safety, reward, and perhaps redemption itself were to be found in one place, more specifically, in one person.

> Consider the lilies of the field, how they grow; they toil not, neither do they spin: And yet I say unto you, That even Solomon in all his glory was not arrayed like one of these. Wherefore, if God so clothe the grass of the field, which today is, and tomorrow is cast into the oven, shall he not much more clothe you, O ye of little faith? Therefore take no thought, saying, What shall we eat? or, What shall we drink? or, Wherewithal shall we be clothed? (For after all these things do the Gentiles seek:) for your heavenly Father knoweth that ye have need of all these things.
>
> But seek ye first the kingdom of God, and his righteousness; and all these things shall be added unto you. Take therefore no thought for the morrow: for the morrow shall take thought for the things of itself. Sufficient unto the day is the evil thereof.
>
> —MATTHEW 6:28-34 KJV

outside the spoil of words

Scripture commends us to pray without ceasing,[3] but I was never sure how this was possible, especially in a world that demands so much of us. The thought of doing anything without ceasing is a little overwhelming, especially something as consuming as prayer can be. It engages the voice, the heart, the will, the mind, the body. We tend to think of prayer as a verbal exercise: a whisper, a shout, a groan. Public, private, meditative, it is something we do, a time we set aside, an action we take. And it is right that we do this and as often as possible.

But as living things can be, prayer is also migratory; it moves with us, it settles upon us outside our awareness. The same prayer that puts words in our mouths also settles somewhere quietly, and at times unquietly within us, in the recesses, beyond the reach of thought. Prayer has life within and beyond us.

Because of this, it is possible for life itself to take on the nature of prayer, outside action or intent, outside the need for speech. Our very lives become the offering we make, continuous, without end, substantial—our thanksgiving, our praise, our petitions—all outside the spoil of words and all within the immense jurisdiction of God's love. He knows our need before we do, while it is still mute and shapeless.

∘ ∘

Before a word is on my tongue
you know it completely, O Lord.

PSALM 139:4

∘ ∘ ∘ ∘ ∘ ∘ ∘ ∘ ∘ ∘ ∘ ∘ ∘ ∘ ∘ ∘ ∘ ∘ ∘ ∘

Think of it as a current of exchange between you and the Almighty—a living current, a giving and receiving, always in a state of flow, just shy of awareness, deeper and more certain than thought, made pure in the very innocence by which it comes. It is a fruitfully honest prayer. It has none of the usual contaminations and comes not in the interruption of life, but in its very flow. It exists outside agenda and maneuvering, outside invention and craft. God loves the sound of your voice and whatever music it makes, but he loves your silence as well; both are alive to him, and both are full with meaning:

> The ever-changing reality in the midst of which we live should
> awaken us to the possibility of an uninterrupted dialogue
> with God. By this I do not mean continuous "talk"…but a
> dialogue of love and of choice. A dialogue of deep wills.
>
> —THOMAS MERTON, *NEW SEEDS OF CONTEMPLATION*

Life in his presence can be conducted at full speed, with all its complications, all its surprises, all its injustice, all its sudden beauty, all its ugliness, all its stretch and pull. The whole liturgy of life, the entire procession, all the lovely and unlovely, all the good and all the not so good. I can work at my job, do the chores asked of me, and with my soul at complete rest, intact, having entrusted it into his keeping. Think of it as something mutual between you and God, an agreement, a living agreement, one that he initiates, that he sustains, that he alone empowers that you may enjoy his light and warmth outside the mechanics of thought.

hound after god

No discussion about life in the presence of God would be complete without hearing from one of its pioneers, a seventeenth-century monk named Brother Lawrence, whose one desire in life was to live in the presence of his master at all times, to seek him with all his heart, and to converse with him always. "Our only business," he said, "is to love and delight ourselves in God."

* * * * * * * * * * * * * * * * * * * *

I have endeavored to act only for him. Whatever becomes of
me, whether I be lost or saved, I will always continue to act
purely for the love of God. I shall have this good at least, that
until death I shall have done all that is in me to love him.

BROTHER LAWRENCE
THE PRACTICE OF THE PRESENCE OF GOD

* * * * * * * * * * * * * * * * * * * *

Like Merton's "dialogue of deep wills," this practice of the presence of God, according to Brother Lawrence, is a "habitual, silent, and private conversation of the soul with God." To establish this conversation, he says it is necessary first to "apply to [God] with diligence," that is, to seek after God with all your strength, to think continually, fondly, and lovingly of him, making war on distraction, to pursue him, better yet, to hound after him. "Leave him not alone," the good brother says and then drifts into a kind of rhapsody: "Adore him continually. Live and die with him. This is the glorious work of a Christian; in a word, this is our profession. If we do not know it, we must learn it."

* *

Praise is the best petition we can make
without having to ask for anything.
DAVID TEEMS
TO LOVE IS CHRIST, JANUARY 16

* *

Brother Lawrence lived a highly disciplined life under strict monastic rule. His workload was intense, and the fact that he was crippled, that he suffered chronic pain from an injury sustained in his youth, made it more intense. Then there are the times to consider. Without the benefit of even the simplest conveniences we usually think of, he ran the monastery kitchen: pots, pans, dishes, oven fires, supply, storage, exacting schedules, hungry monks and abbots. Still, he said his set times of prayer were no different from other times because even his most involved labors did not distract his attention from God.

His prayer never ended. It was the prop that supported life.

While he doesn't necessarily make it sound easy or even painless, and he would be the first to say it has a price, nonetheless, speaking with as much enthusiasm as he does authority, Brother Lawrence makes living in the presence of God sound natural, as if it is the happy state of the believer. I'm not sure the apostle Paul would have commended us to pray without ceasing had it not been at first possible and had there not been something about our true nature that he understood.

* * * * * * * * * * * * * * * * * * *

When we are faithful to keep ourselves in his holy presence,
and set him always before us, this hinders our offending him
and doing anything that may displease him. It also begets in
us a holy freedom, and, if I may so speak, a familiarity with
God, where, when we ask, he supplies the grace we need.
Over time, by often repeating these acts, they become habitual,
and the presence of God becomes quite natural to us.

BROTHER LAWRENCE
THE PRACTICE OF THE PRESENCE OF GOD

* * * * * * * * * * * * * * * * * * *

Having God, he wanted more of God. Brother Lawrence resolved to expel anything from his life that was *not* God. He thought of nothing but "how to become wholly God's," to "give the all for the All." He drove from his mind any distraction that frustrated thoughts of God. To be fair, he said this "caused no small pain." Even as the dog has room in his heart for one master, this monk agrees that we must make room there because God fills it to excess with himself.

* * * * * * * * * * * * * * * * * *

The heart must be empty of all other things because God
will possess the heart alone. As he cannot possess it alone
without emptying it of all besides, so, neither can he act there
and do in it what he pleases, unless it be left vacant to him.

BROTHER LAWRENCE
THE PRACTICE OF THE PRESENCE OF GOD

* * * * * * * * * * * * * * * * * *

In *New Seeds of Contemplation,* Thomas Merton, referring to the heart as a sanctuary, says much the same thing:

It is a terrible breaking and burning of idols, a purification of the sanctuary, so that no graven thing may occupy the place that God has commanded to be left empty.

Brother Lawrence was a lowly, unassuming man—a simple man,

a man of great love, a surrendered and selfless man, a humble man "of rough appearance," who pursued God, "not from the head but from the heart." He describes himself as "a footman who was clumsy and broke everything." I am not sure why, but I am reminded of a large, lumbering, but gentle creature of loyal and eager disposition, irrepressibly joyful. A large black Newfoundland perhaps, squeezed into dimensions that cannot possibly contain him, making all rooms small rooms, having about him infinitely more life than space to put it in. Brother Lawrence would have made a great dog.

I temper my playfulness with caution and with awe. For there is neither laughter so deep nor devotion so true as to be found in the lives of those lovers of God like Brother Lawrence or even Francis of Assisi. They are among our best models.

Francis stripped himself clean of his former life to embrace the life of God. With a happy heart he exchanged privilege for privation and necessity, all in the name of love. At the center of his new life he not only found himself, but he found immense joy as well. Like Brother Lawrence, Francis was known for merriment, for laughter and song. He too understood something about the deeper, truer nature of man, and operated within its authority. Francis, the gentle saint who tamed the wolf of Gubbio, who spoke the creature down from his madness with a word, delivering both a town and the beast that tormented it. "Come to me, Brother Wolf."[4]

at home with awe

Each of these men, and countless others who were deeply immersed in the presence of God, was well aware that it could take speech and breath from them. In Scripture we see that the presence of God, the glory that surrounds him, has an almost physical texture about it.[5] To the ancients, the very name of God carried so much presence, the awe was so overwhelming, they refused to say it or spell it. Daniel, the prophet, the Old Testament revelator who sat unmoved among lions, whose wisdom ruled a foreign people, in the presence of God, said,

I am overcome with anguish because of the vision, my lord,

and I am helpless. How can I, your servant, talk with you,
my lord? My strength is gone and I can hardly breathe.

—DANIEL 10:16-17

Isaiah saw the Lord, and dared not approach without a touch of
dread:

Woe is me! for I am undone; because I am a man of unclean
lips, and I dwell in the midst of a people of unclean lips: for
mine eyes have seen the King, the LORD of hosts.

—ISAIAH 6:5 KJV

Love will leave us speechless at times. It makes us aware of its
power—the one good tug on a leash that reminds me who is master and who is not. It is this living awe that teaches me, that trains
and comforts me, that holds me fast. It is as tender as it is mighty. It
gives me an understanding of just who I am. It overcomes and qui-
ets me. It shepherds my soul about—into the workplace, into all the
theaters of life. It directs my paths. It distills into my hands, into
my speech, into all transactions I make with life around me. I am at
home with awe.

● ● ● ● ● ● ● ● ● ● a prayer of presence ● ● ● ● ● ● ● ● ●

And what would I ask? That I might live in the pleasure of the Lord all my
days? That I might lose myself in his deep contentment? That I might know
the kindness that moves his heart? That I might love what he loves? To
know where his approval lies, his consent, and where it doesn't? To trust
when there is no sense of him? To know his voice as clear as I know my
own, to discern his voice among the multitude of voices? That my life might
be caught up like a prayer, washed clean of doubt and misbelief, of all
traces of mortality? That my prayer, like my heart, be relieved of so many
questions? Do with me as you please, Lord. My abandonment knows no
limit. Let there be no restraints to my joy—the wild, shameless, idiot joy,
the dance in me I cannot restrain, the very carnival of love. My senses
ache for want of you.

In Christ, master, the one voice I discern among the many, Christ, till kindness is lord over action, and Christ, till I have no holds in this life, no claims to make. Amen.

May God's presence become everything to you.
May the sound of his voice, his approaching footsteps,
and the very sound of his name
start a happy riot in your soul.

it's almost like being in love

*It is a dreadful thing to fall into the
hands of the living God.*

HEBREWS 10:31

*I have no punishment to fear;
But, ah! That smile from thee
Imparts a pang far more severe
Than woe itself would be.*

MADAME JEANNE GUYON
DIVINE JUSTICE

*The heart that is free of love sickness isn't
a heart at all. The body deprived of the pangs of love
is nothing but clay and water.*

JAMI
TWELFTH-CENTURY PERSIAN MYSTIC

I T WAS NOTICEABLE WITH ALL THREE OF THE DOGS. When we gave any one of them individual attention, particularly if it included soft words and gentle strokes to the crown of the head, changes occurred in their features—physiological changes made evident on the surface, inward events that could neither be controlled nor concealed. All motion ceased, at least all visible motion, with possible exception of the tail, which kept a slower time, sweeping gently in the adagio of love. Panting slowed. The eyes softened and all the features seemed to melt into some degree of bliss.

As a family we were liberal with our affection. Where love needed a voice, we did our best to give it one. We were not afraid to touch, and we held back nothing from each other. After all, ours was a house of little boys and dogs. From pups they were always falling over each other with that romp and nibble that taught them the limits, that gave them a sense of big dog/little dog, and taught them how to live in community.

> As young dogs, life was all exploration and wonder, awe and adventure, curiosity and scramble—things we might say about love itself.

The same could be said of the dogs.

As young dogs, life was all exploration and wonder, awe and adventure, curiosity and scramble—things we might say about love itself. Like life, it was eager and untiring, as it always is, as I suppose it had to be. The attachments they were capable of would last a lifetime. As the dogs got older, and as that sense of community flourished, love prospered in the midst of us. It became fluent and grew to the dimensions we enjoyed together.

Our dogs figured out early that love was most readily available at the top of our little structure, that seasoned love was the best love, the most consistent love. Adam and Shad could be as aloof as pups sometimes. Of course, the dogs loved that about them. So did we, for that matter. Their energies were all very similar. The dogs cherished time with our sons, but the greater part of their devotion defaulted to Benita and me.

The dogs had a good sense of us. They seemed to understand the economy of our attention, how to get it and how to keep it, who was good for it, who was not. We were ever the object of their interests. Time spent with us bred confidence in them, and if the dogs were anything, they were confident—amusingly, harmlessly, and above all, warmly confident. They were not afraid to make demands of us.

During any given petting spree, if we took too long of a pause between strokes or if we got a bit too distracted with something else, they made their annoyance conspicuous. Negotiation took many forms. The first round was usually a gentle tap with a paw, a reminder that "Hey, I am here, and I am patient. You may resume at any time."

Next, they might sit and stare at us until we caught on, shifting their weight on their front legs slightly from side to side in anticipation. At some point the snout would get involved. A nudge here, there. The last resort was to bark or, in Savannah's case, groan. They were very good at this type of command, and though slow at times, we were fairly good at compliance. The bark was not a very large bark. It was more of an aggravated cough mixed with a bit of complaining howl, but it was always friendly fire, and always playful. We loved the music it made.

The dogs understood mutuality and connectedness as well, if not better, than we did. "You have ignored me too long. A good walk would do us both good!" Or the usual, "I haven't had a good belly rub in days. I know you're good for it, and I know how much it means to you. I know you enjoy this as much as I do." They were right. We were good for it.

Love had such a good sense about it, and there was such a bright and casual intelligence awakened between us, it was easy to overlook the true wonder of it. The distinction between master and dog seemed to disappear, though the very strength of our relationship was founded upon that distinction. And this is the whole point of worship, is it not? Love's whole idea is union, the lightness of true possession.

as a flower expands under the sun

Their devotion was unquestionable. It was always *on,* always vibrant. They lived too genuinely, too close to the truth, for anything less. Though I can hope otherwise, they were better at being devoted than I was at being master. They made me look good.

A good master gives all the cues. He sets the borders in place. He determines the standards of exchange. Judgment and contentment, validation and consent are all in his keeping. He becomes the template by which love and union find their shape. He determines the degree of warmth and accessibility. I am not sure how easy you and I make it for God, but I am pretty sure the same conditions apply.

• • • • • • • • • • • • • • • • • • •

Unless He utters Himself in you, speaks His own name
in the center of your soul, you will no more know Him
than a stone knows the ground upon which it rests.

THOMAS MERTON
NEW SEEDS OF CONTEMPLATION

• • • • • • • • • • • • • • • • • • •

The following account beautifully describes the transformation of a dog overcome with love for his master (or god):

> White Fang was in the process of finding himself. In spite of the maturity of his years and of the savage rigidity of the mould that had formed him, his nature was undergoing an expansion…His old code of conduct was changing.
>
> Like had been replaced by love. And love was the plummet dropped down into the deeps of him where like had never gone. And responsive out of his deeps had come the new thing—love. That which was given unto him did he return. This was a god indeed, a love-god, a warm and radiant god, in whose light White Fang's nature expanded as a flower expands under the sun…
>
> His love partook of the nature of worship, dumb, inarticulate, a silent adoration. Only by the steady regard of his eyes did he express his love, and by the unceasing following with his eyes of his god's every movement. Also, at times, when his god looked at him and spoke to him, he betrayed an awkward self-consciousness, caused by the struggle of his love to express itself and his physical inability to express it.
>
> —JACK LONDON, *WHITE FANG*

What London suggests is that in love a truer version of ourselves is possible. Deep nature is aroused and summoned upward, outward. What the animal felt for his master (his god) stirred in his depths so completely, so thoroughly, as to rid him of his former rule, his former imperatives, indeed, his former life, subject to a new rule as he now was.

Everything changes. *Everything.* All former contracts are either broken or revised under this new rule. The old foundation is set aside for a more permanent one. Nature at last, that deep silent forgotten nature in each of us, has a chance to expand, to discover itself, to show something true to a world so in need of the authentic.

Nothing will look the same again. The light changes. It intensifies and illumines. Belief itself will clarify. And simplify. The old forms will lose their appeal. Be warned. You will not be able to go back to the way it was before. It is not unlike a banishment from your former life. The same apostle who said *"God is love"* also said, *"God is light."*[1]

* *

When perfection comes, the imperfect disappears.

1 CORINTHIANS 13:10

* *

The path to authenticity begins in love. Love brings with it liberation from all counterfeits and imitations. It may or may not happen all at once, but we are nonetheless groomed by love itself—washed, fed, and nurtured. The old mirrors no longer satisfy. The old mythology goes quiet and speaks no more. The original script emerges—deeper, truer, accurate.

It is not difficult to see how God is jealous concerning our authentic self—how important it is to him. Holiness is merely being who we are. Anything else is a distortion of his design, a mockery of his finest achievement.

* *

There is a momentum the heart will follow when it finds it, an impulse, an irresistible drift, a current upon which it may yield and free itself, a stream that runs in a single direction, a cadence by which we may know our true step, a tide that may cradle and carry us, a propensity that is soul specific, that has your name and His seal upon it, by a script written in a careful hand. It tells us who we are in a world of phantoms. It gives us singularity and selfhood in a world

of masked men. And it is along this path we find the little
evidences of our homeland, that thing that haunts the soul.

DAVID TEEMS
TO LOVE IS CHRIST, JANUARY 7

• • • • • • • • • • • • • • • • • • • •

Most of us live according to the myths we grew up on. Our lives take shape around them. Some are pleasant, some unpleasant, but either way they are fiction. And if we live outside the truth, if we live according to our illusions even innocently, our perceptions, our judgments, our desires are all contaminated, spoiled.

To live outside truth is to misperceive God, and if our perception of God is distorted, nothing can be clear to us. All life is askew. We may be saved, but we live just shy of the redemption we could be enjoying daily, continuously. To deny God in the least part of him is to deny him all. To overturn such a life, half measures will not do.

love is absolute

I'm not sure a dog understands half measures or half efforts. The middle way is not attractive to her. She is led by a simple faith that gives simple options. *Yes* and *no* are sufficient.[2] *On* or *off.* One thing and not the other. This is what she understands.

First Corinthians 13 pays homage to the two words "always" and "never." There is no middle way for this pair. No gray between the black and the white, no "almost" or "maybe" to cripple the resolve:

> [Love] always protects, always trusts, always hopes, always perseveres. Love never fails.

—1 CORINTHIANS 13:7-8

Love is an absolute. Love is comfortable in the presence of absolutes. That is why you hear adjectives such as "unconditional" attached to it. Unconditional love is a state of completeness for which there is no negotiation, no option.

Both noun and adjective, "absolute" is one of the most challenged words of our time. Standing counter to an age that has little use for it anymore, it is an unattractive word politically and culturally. Yet it refuses to go away.

* * * * * * * * * * * * * * * * * * * *

"Absolute": Free from conditions or reservations; unreserved, unqualified, unconditional. Existing without relation to any other being; self-existent; self-sufficing. Capable of being thought or conceived by itself alone; unconditioned.

OXFORD ENGLISH DICTIONARY

* * * * * * * * * * * * * * * * * * * *

It also means "absolved, disengaged, unfettered, detached," suggesting independence, separated out, or standing alone. It suggests quality or degree; "free from all imperfection or deficiency; complete, finished; perfect, consummate." We also use the word "absolute" concerning the nature of rule:

> Marked by freedom from restraint or control by any governing or commanding agent or instrumentality: having supreme power effectively or formally without constitutional or other restrictions: marked by extreme concentration of complete power and jurisdiction.

—OXFORD ENGLISH DICTIONARY

The devoted life will demand that we come to terms with such a word, to be at peace with it in spite of the times. It is not a permissive or compromising word. It is not a compliant word. It does not bend easily. But for our purposes, it is a very useful word. Surrender that is absolute is a perfect surrender, a complete surrender, free from all imperfection or deficiency, washed clean, free from half measures, a surrender that gives itself no options.

In Eden, man was more at home with absolutes. He thought little of it. He was at home with divinity, at home with God, at home with himself. His nakedness before God was absolute. It was complete, perfect.

Death is an absolute. Dead is dead. There is no half measure. Though the cliché is popular, and though one might be extremely tired, there is no "half dead." Even so, and against all this finality, love is stronger than death. It is more powerful, more preeminent than death. Only love can rob death of its power, of its very absoluteness. This is true of love in any of its forms. This is true of death, for that matter, in any of its forms. We could say love is stronger than negation. It is possible to *outlove* malevolence, to *outlove* injustice and evil intent, to *outlove* the critical spirit and render it silent.

> Love's whole idea is union, the lightness of true possession.

Where love is not reciprocated, it has to be longer, wider; it has to have more reach. It must rally all its superlatives, all its best qualities where it meets the greatest resistance.

A dog can love a brutal master with just as much unconditional love as she can a benign one. Cruelty is an outward expression of an inward condition. If by living an authentic life the dog has a clearer sense of what is authentic, she may have some sense of her master not evident to the rest of us—or even to the master himself. Seeing purely, she is able to love purely in keeping with love's own standard. She is able to love her master beyond the cruelty, beyond the injustice of the moment.

The same is possible for any of us. We can love mean people. We can love the bitter, the abusers. We can love beyond the smallness of others. We can love beneath the hardened surfaces, meet difficult psychologies with advantage and without fear. If we live by truth, truth becomes more evident to us. Jeffrey Masson makes this boast on the dog's behalf:

> Questers of the truth, that's who dogs are; seekers after the invisible scent of another being's authentic core.
>
> —DOGS NEVER LIE ABOUT LOVE

For this reason, it is possible for the dog to love us more than we love ourselves. Her vision is not distorted. She is unaffected by the illusions we honor concerning ourselves. They mean nothing to her. She sees beyond them—beyond the insulation, beyond the myth. Love and truth labor together in the dog's behalf to clarify her perception. She indeed may know us better than we know ourselves. We may know only the image. She knows the substance behind it.

This is speculation, of course, but the argument is a strong one. This would explain the depth of her conviction. Anyway, the dog has given herself no options. She doesn't allow half measures because she doesn't understand them.

To love in truth is to love as God loves—to love purely, absolutely, to see as he sees. Love looks beyond the imaginary, beyond the legends, beyond the person we merely think we see, to the person who is actually there.

a most unfortunate queen

If dogs celebrate love with all their might, they grieve its loss with the same intensity. It is a vow they honor without question. When love is interrupted or when death intervenes, when that connection between dog and master is threatened or severed, they are not afraid to grieve—and to grieve hard. They seem to understand that grief is no less a celebration of love. It just hurts more.

The dog knows herself well enough to have no doubt about what she feels. She can feel without restraint, and she does just that. Love grants all the permission necessary. This has been proven again and again historically. The following tale demonstrates the power of the attachment between dog and master. It concerns a most unfortunate queen.

In 1587, Mary Queen of Scots was executed for treason under Elizabeth I. Mary was the mother of James VI of Scotland, who eventually succeeded Elizabeth on the throne of England and became James I, the king who gave us the Bible that goes by his name. It was a rather wacky time.

Mary had a little dog, a Maltese. Her husband was assassinated, her only child taken from her at one year old; other than a few royal attendants, the dog was her intimate companion through many years of house arrest. History does not give us the name of the dog,[3] only the record of its devotion. At last, awaiting trial in Fotheringay Castle, the dog was her one solace against the madness that would eventually take her life.

On the morning of her execution, she walked rather slowly to the block. While you and I might have done the same thing, this was not due to fear. Mary considered herself a martyr for her faith and accepted death graciously. The pace she kept was for the sake of the little dog hidden within the confusion of her petticoats. It was a comfort to have the dog near.

The account of the execution is rather grim, but after his work was done, the executioner noticed movement in Mary's dress—the dog. Dappled with blood, the dog refused to be taken from its dead master.

Because of the testimony the creature made and the sympathy it would arouse, the powers-that-be wanted the dog out of England—banished or worse. A French princess claimed the dog. It was to live in a palace again, with all the advantages of royalty. The dog was not impressed. Its heart was too full. It died only weeks after Mary's execution. It was said the creature grieved to death.

Dogs don't merely play at love. They actually mean it. That is why it is such a lovely spectacle of nature. One author writes, "A dog is utterly sincere. It cannot pretend."[4] Perhaps that is the real reason we enjoy them so much, simply because their thought life isn't quite the tangle ours seem to be. They demand nothing from me but me.

- - - - - - - - - - - - - - - - - - - -

Dogs do not lie to you about how they feel
because they cannot lie about feelings.

JEFFREY MASSON
DOGS NEVER LIE ABOUT LOVE

- - - - - - - - - - - - - - - - - - - -

we will make a kind of happiness

Devotion is not a game to the dog. She takes it seriously. She is vigilant. She seems to know how it works and why it is important. Devotion is visceral. It defines her. It makes the awe of nature visible, almost audible, telling quite profoundly of a Creator that stashes bits of himself in all he creates and who defines himself by one thing— love. Every action he takes has that one life behind it. It is the single motive in his heart.

The dog also sets no limits on who is worthy of her love. Forgive my presumption, but the dog exercises a radical Christianity that observes no preference whatsoever. Her love is not colored with bias or preferment. Her love has no politics. It knows neither rank nor station. She can love at either end of the social horizon with just as much veracity and fearlessness, just as much joy and bubble. Beggar, prince, new money, old money, no money, it matters as little to the dog as it does to God. One poet wrote:

> I sing the mangy dog, the pitiful, the homeless dog, the roving dog, the circus dog…I sing the luckless dog who wanders alone through the winding ravines of huge cities, or the one who blinks up at some poor outcast of society with its soulful eyes, as much as to say, "take me with you, and out of our joint misery we will make a kind of happiness."

—CHARLES BAUDELAIRE, *"THE FAITHFUL DOG," PARIS SPLEEN*

According to authentic faith, am I to give as much as my very life for a stranger? The hard answer is *yes*. Am I to love to the extent of my own ruin if so asked? The same hard answer. Unreasonable, illogical, love this extreme is possible only to one who is lost so completely in God as to have no identity outside him. Truth is, one loses nothing because God cannot be lost. Outside him, there is not strength enough, nor divinity enough, nor desire enough to love.

This sacrifice of self is the highest form worship can take. In the devoted life, martyrdom is a daily event. The following questions, while not the easiest for any of us to answer, are necessary nonetheless.

Is my soul yet purged of waste and distraction? Is it yet free of smallness and complaint? Can I love a beggar or a prince with the same full heart? Is my love so like God's as to be sacrificial? Would I give my heart away simply because he asks me to? Can I cast it off as if it were a trifle? Or is my

Christianity a mere painting of love, an image to reverence and pay small homage to, something outside the flow of life, outside relevance itself?

Do I reserve my worship for a given time and place? Is it bound to a certain style or protocol? Or is my worship migratory? Does it wake with me in the morning, smile upon me throughout the course of my day, give me words when I need them, courage in a time of indecision? Does worship gather me up at night? Is it still warm on my lips when sleep comes over me at last? Am I lost in you, Lord, or am I just lost?

These questions suggest a love that is severe. But is there any other kind?

This brings us back to the dog. *Joyful, joyful, joyful!* In all creation below man there is no more intense lover than the dog, and there is perhaps no creature happier. She is sold out. Devotion *is* life to her. She has rediscovered her paradise.

And she knows her redeemer. She studies him. She aches in the absence of him. Sometimes she aches in his presence. Without worship even the dog knows life is missing something necessary, something written on nature itself.

• • • • • • • • • • • • • • • • •

I abandoned and forgot myself
Laying my face on my beloved;
All things ceased; I went out from myself
Leaving my cares
Forgotten among the lilies.

JOHN OF THE CROSS
THE ASCENT TO MOUNT CARMEL

• • • • • • • • • • • • • • • • •

the love that imparadises life

Love has grown somewhat pale in our time, anemic. It has weakened under our abuses. With our usual gift for excess and self-absorption, love has been dethroned, or at least consigned to a lesser seat. We have trivialized love. We live in a world afraid to touch, a world sterilizing itself, taking care to use gloves on all it handles.

As a culture, we have lost faith in absolutes. In such a culture, in such a world, true love becomes the rare exception. We feed on substitutes, having lost our taste for the original. A saccharine love.

In the fallout, we have become strangers to our own nature, to the deep reserves of self. We have lost that creature confidence in God that made love a way of life for the fathers and mothers of our faith. They were wild for it. Love was too large, too unwieldy, too immediate, too present to be confined to a building or to bear any other name than that of its master, Christ. The townsfolk thought they were intoxicated.[5] I suppose they were. It was the wine in their blood.

A desperate love, it gave Christianity a beginning.

It is little wonder that Peter could preach and get the numbers he got in response. Was it eloquence? Possibly. After all, he had turned poet-prophet under the apprenticeship of Christ. Was it charm? Probably not. Was it celebrity, personal charisma, presence? Somehow I doubt it. That might work for him today, but back then? No, it was something else, something higher, something fervently alive, something white hot, wild, and uncivilized that gave him words that day. They had little defense against it. "And the same day there were added unto them about three thousand souls" (Acts 2:41).

The same love that put firebrands into the mouth of John the Baptist also freed the man of the tombs, put gratitude on his tongue instead of curses, serenity in his mind where there had been only madness. He *came to himself* (which is the entire point). He gathered with confidence at his master's feet.[6]

> The sacrifice of self is the highest form worship can take. In the devoted life, martyrdom is a daily event.

King David was so smitten, his heart so overcharged, his joy so rampant and immediate, he threw off all restraints.[7] Savannah would actually turn in ecstatic little circles before me, dizzy with love. Like David, she didn't care what anyone thought. She couldn't help herself.

Things are different now. We are all grown up. Or so we tell ourselves. *Agape* is just Greek to most of us. We live in an indulgent age, an age of options—options that past generations could not foresee or perhaps even imagine. We have been given option upon option, and more options, choices, more choices, and even more choices. This is not necessarily a bad thing, but the effects are rather conspicuous. For some, it causes a type of paralysis. The sheer volume of choices makes it impossible to choose at all. It becomes easier to just follow the herd.

Through mismanagement or misbelief, fear, or perhaps countless failures, we have given ourselves options in love as well. But the image of a thing is not the thing itself, and the illusion of love, in spite of how comfortable we have become with it, is not the reality. The sad thing is, we hardly know the difference anymore.

We can be thankful that God remains patient with us, that he is ever teaching us through his creation, through his creatures, and in our case through something as silly and at once as beautiful as the dog. We should be grateful that God is ever showing us the path to heaven, the one we might enjoy here on earth, that we have access to in love—not the illusion, nor the imagined likeness, but true love, the inspired kind of love, the one that has the seal of divinity stamped on it, the love that imparadises life.

Of course, if my dogs were with me at this moment, I would be preaching to the choir.

● ● ● ● ● ● ● ●   prayer for those in love   ● ● ● ● ● ● ● ●

It is a dreadful thing, an awesome thing, a wonderfully terrible thing to fall into the hands of the Living God—warm and comforting. And let me fall. For I am in love too steep. Let me trust the hands that made me, the hands that bled for my release. Awaken what sleeps in me. I want to be accessible, touchable, reachable. I want to be available, pliable. Let me rejoice with those who rejoice. Let me grieve with those who grieve, that their sorrow becomes my sorrow, their joy my joy. Put dominion in me. Let love rule and give instruction. Let love be conspicuous—the first evidence of my faith. Let my heart glow with love's great heat that this too dull and loveless world may brighten in its overflow. Give me the wisdom, Lord, to recognize and the strength to shake off what is artificial in me, the hollow, lifeless forms of love. Until my heart is free. Until I love my neighbor as myself. Until celebration stirs within my limbs.

In Christ, where life and love mingle as in a common cup. Amen.

As it was with David, may God love to watch you dance,
to be your absolute and unguarded self.

4

saint bernard

The reason for loving God is God.

BERNARD OF CLAIRVAUX
ON LOVING GOD

What language shall I borrow to thank thee, dearest friend,
For this thy dying sorrow, thy pity without end?
O make me thine forever; and should I fainting be,
Lord, let me never, never outlive my love for thee.

BERNARD OF CLAIRVAUX
O, SACRED HEAD, NOW WOUNDED

Que me amat, amet et canem meum. (Love me, love my dog.)

BERNARD OF CLAIRVAUX
SERMO PRIMUS

LOVE ME, LOVE MY DOG." When I read those words I knew I had the right guy. I think my dogs would have immediately liked him. And with a name like Saint Bernard, well, he is one of us. He was a frail but outrageously inspired and energetic little monk who loved so purely and with so much of himself he would forget to eat.[1] Bernard of Clairvaux (1090–1153) is one of the better examples of the devoted life history has bequeathed to us. He went at it with a severity you and I may never be asked, pioneering new territory of thought and devotion as he did, but there are elements of his life and his teaching that are indispensable, that make it worth our time to step outside our metaphor just a moment.

If you seek God with any degree of honest passion, if you love God with an intense love, if you find that love is at the heart of what you believe about him, if love is the way you perceive faith itself and choose to invest yourself or to give yourself away, if you seek God in the heart of your neighbor and find that you love them for it, for finding him there, then an encounter with Bernard is not only beneficial, it is somewhat inevitable.

By the way, the legendary dog is named for an altogether different Bernard.[2] Still, I love the image it makes—the large, bounding, heroic, risk-taking, persevering creature that loves beyond itself to save others. Sounds a lot like our guy: writer and holy man, mystic and hymn-maker, poet and preacher of the Crusades, priest to the Knights Templar, defender of the faith, counselor to popes and kings, a contemplative and the father of contemplatives, founder of monasteries, a friend to Eleanor of Aquitaine (the mother of *Coeur de Lion*, Richard the Lion-heart), Abbott of Clairvaux, lover of God and men.

In appearance, he was, at best, understated, and yet he could rattle abbey walls with the bright pounding hammer of his speech. He was an inspired pulpiteer, articulate and incendiary, as precise as he was provocative. If he had a poet's heart, and he did, he also had a warrior's heart—the prophet in sackcloth, the gentle soul aflame with the life of God. He could preach kingdoms down, and then turn and write a song that would make you weep for its sweetness. Next time you hear "O, Sacred Head, Now Wounded" or "Jesus, the Very Thought of Thee," think of Bernard.

*   *   *   *   *   *   *   *   *   *   *   *   *   *   *

Jesus, the very thought of Thee
With sweetness fills my breast;
But sweeter far Thy face to see
And in Thy presence rest.
BERNARD OF CLAIRVAUX

*   *   *   *   *   *   *   *   *   *   *   *   *   *   *

In his youth, he fed on the works of Horace, Plato, Aristotle, Virgil, and Ovid. His instructors saw something in Bernard that was special, and years later, once he fell hard in love with God and wanting his nakedness before his God to be complete, he attempted to shoo it all away, to deny that part of him that had grown lyrical. God would not let him. Nor would his superiors.

He had become literary, and in spite of himself, the young monk became a writer of serious weight. He wrote with persuasion and grandeur, with a fertile lyricism and a soft, natural thunder. Pope Pius XII (1953) noted that Bernard's style is "animated, rich, smooth, and characterized by vivid language, is filled with such pleasing unction it attracts, delights, and raises to heavenly things the mind of the reader. It arouses, nourishes, and strengthens piety; it spurs the soul to the pursuit of those good things which are not passing or transitory, but true, certain, and everlasting."[3]

He was a lover and student of Scripture. It was his meat and drink. And in all his activity, inward and outward, love was his center of gravity.

• • • • • • • • • • • • • • • • • • •

What would be the good of learning without love? It would puff us up. And love without learning? It would go astray.

BERNARD OF CLAIRVAUX
SERMON 69, CANTICLE OF CANTICLES

• • • • • • • • • • • • • • • • • • •

He was born in a castle near Dijon, France. He was born to wealth and status and a great name. But like the gentle Francis who would come not long after him, Bernard renounced his holdings to take upon himself the livery of God, expressed by the very poverty he loved. His nakedness before God, like that of Francis of Assisi, is profound at many levels.

Bernard stripped himself not only of the wealth he was born into, but of all counterfeits, all weights and encumbrances—anything that separated him from his first love, which was God alone. In the process Bernard learned what it meant to be Bernard.

• • • • • • • • • • • • • • • • • • • •

Bernard made a sign to me, and smiled,
telling me to look higher.

DANTE ALIGHIERI
"PARADISO," THE DIVINE COMEDY

• • • • • • • • • • • • • • • • • • •

He knew God had shaped him for his own pleasure, and he became pliable, soft in the hands of his beloved master. Having been divested of all that was *not* Bernard, he was, like our friend the dog, quintessentially himself. Bernard of Clairvaux will help us further clarify what the devoted life is and what it will ask of you and me.

Like my dogs, Bernard makes the devoted life look easy. *Is he relevant? Is he current? Are there too many years between us, too much dust?* Yes, yes, and no. He is both relevant and current. In spite of the 800 years or so, it seems only right to speak of Bernard in the present tense. He is rather deathless.

a man in love

"So take from my poverty what I can give you." It sounds like something I might have written in my journals years ago, or maybe just this morning. It has the resonance of a vow, one you might make to God or to someone you love deeply. When asked by his superiors to answer the question why God is to be loved, those were among Bernard's first words. There is a slight reluctance in the tone, but he accepted the commission, and I, for one, am glad he did.

It was a brief piece of work he simply called *On Loving God.* Both simple and profound, it is a necessary key to help us understand what lies at the heart of the devoted life.

According to Bernard, if God is love, then to be *in God,* is to be *in love.* For once, the math is easy. Is he a man in love? It sure sounds like it to me. He has one thing on his mind. Like London's White Fang, our Saint Bernard has room in his heart for only one master. He knows his master well, and therefore he preaches possibility, he preaches the attainable God.

You and I were created to love. This is the warm center of Bernard's message. It is also the founding principle of the devoted life—that we live according to that for which we were created. It means love has mastery over life, dominion and precedence as it did in our beginnings. Everything he writes implies origin.

- -

[God] hath endowed us with the possibility of love.
BERNARD OF CLAIRVAUX
ON LOVING GOD

- -

Love is the great fix of broken things, yes, but also of misprized, disregarded, neglected things. Love repairs deep memory. Life can be what it was intended to be, that is, life without the stops, without the hesitations or denials, life at its first and finest. Not to rewrite the Scripture, but to make it louder, we might read it this way:

> I [Christ, love incarnate, love in person, God made warm
> and visible] have come that they may have life, and have it
> to the full.
>
> —JOHN 10:10

But *why* love God? Bernard's answer is lucid, and delightfully simple:

> You want me to tell you why God is to be loved and how
> much. I answer, the reason for loving God is God himself;
> and the measure of love due to him is immeasurable love.
> Is this plain?
>
> —BERNARD OF CLAIRVAUX, *ON LOVING GOD*

Is this plain? Ouch. As if he wonders why his superiors had to ask in the first place. "*Why should we love God?*" they ask. "*Duh!*" says the monk. If you compare the language of this one essay against his many sermons you cannot help but notice the lack of ornament. He makes it very plain. And I am grateful. It cannot be plain enough.

on loving God

God fashioned the heart of man so there would be no satisfaction in anything but himself. *Things* never satisfy. *Things* cannot satisfy—whether it be a great name, wealth, celebrity, great holdings, toys. The truest satisfaction a man can know is union with God. It is more than mere friendship, remembering that God himself chose the metaphor, the image of the lover and the beloved, the bride and bridegroom.

If it is true that the cause for loving God is God, it is also true that the reward for loving God is also God. He is his own reward. Bernard says the same is true of love itself: "True love is its own reward."

• •

Love is a mystery that we may live out. Like God, love is its own explanation, the riddle and its answer. Love gives no tongue to explain itself anymore than God, and yet we can enjoy Him and live in Him and find our sufficiency, our completeness in Him. Like love itself, He is His own reward. He is His own explanation. There are things for which knowing does not apply. Love is one of them. It is a mystery and yet one that explains as much as it hides.

DAVID TEEMS
TO LOVE IS CHRIST, FEBRUARY 28

• •

It is my own doing, I admit it. But I am deeply attracted to the notion of being *in love* as a way to clarify my faith. It helps me adjust my sights, to reorder and refine perspective. It makes my faith suddenly that much more personal, intimate. It lifts it out of obscurity, out of the domain of theology into something more accessible, even as Christ put heaven within my reach. *I am in love.* Can I tell you about my faith? *I am in love.*

When I first met my wife, riot broke out. There was no way to harness what I felt, and it came upon me with all the validations of heaven. Who am I kidding? Outside of God himself, it was as close as I had ever been to heaven...or it seemed so. Love meddled with me deeply, shook me to my foundations. My speech, as well as my thoughts, turned lyrical. There was no plain text. Love had to sing for it was anything but quiet. My breathing altered. And looking back, my first response to God was not much different. It followed a similar progression. Love does that, and at levels within each of us we are hardly aware.

• • • • • • • • • • • • • • • • • • • •

At that moment, and what I say is true, the vital spirit, the one that dwells in the most secret chamber of the heart, began to tremble so violently that even the least pulses of my body were strangely affected; and trembling, it spoke these words: "Here is a god stronger than I, who shall come to rule over me."

DANTE ALIGHIERI
VITA NUOVA, C. 1292–1294

• • • • • • • • • • • • • • • • • • • •

Rule over me indeed. This is an extraordinary way to say it perhaps, to say I am in love, but it is the way I happen to explain my faith, how I have come to understand it. It puts the command of Christ, the command to love, right up front, above all other considerations of belief. Love is all the theology necessary. Indeed, it moves theology out of the foreground and puts something brighter and truer, something more significant and more godlike in its place.

Again, to be *in God* is to be *in love*. We can talk theology and other curiosities of thought, but love is the only issue. I enjoy all the advantages, all the amenities of being in love—the elevated thought life, the unstoppable lyricism, the life of pure possibility, the warm anticipation of presence that lovers know, the power that imposes divinity on all trails of life.

I can live my life in all its ordinariness as if background music were playing.

I do not mean to beguile or misdirect you with clever-sounding argument, or to suggest some life that is rather impossible. On the contrary, this is all too real. This is life at its *most* genuine. The *me* that is most authentic. The *me* I like the best.

Does this diminish God somehow? Does it make something less

of him or his holiness? No, it does not. On the contrary, love elevates man, gives him access to heaven—the one he was meant to enjoy here on earth, now, fully. To live in God, to live in union with him, to live in agreement with him, is to share heaven, to regain an earthly paradise, that lovely confusion of realms.

Does such a life explain all the mysteries? No. The mystery of God remains intact—beautiful, impenetrable, and, above all, interesting. The devoted life is a life of surrender, of absolute trust, trust when reason says other things, when the arguments in your head make better sense, trust when you have no real sense of him. The mysteries themselves are absorbed into the ordinary flow of life, making ordinary life anything but ordinary.

> I suddenly find God in places I did not expect to find him. I commune with him everywhere. I enjoy a new taste and a new awareness of his omnipresence.

Bernard found this to be true, and once he did, he sold the farm. He jettisoned his old life—all traces of it, all of his holdings for this new one.

This condition is all-inclusive, and the obligation it imposes is sweet. I suddenly find God in places I did not expect to find him. I commune with him everywhere. I enjoy a new taste and a new awareness of his omnipresence. For instance, if God loves my neighbor, and he does, if he abides in my neighbor's heart, I should all the more love my neighbor in search of him. I can commune with God through my neighbor and love my neighbor as commanded. My neighbor becomes a gate, a passage, a portal into the divine.

Suddenly the command of Christ makes even deeper sense. Loving God and loving my neighbor becomes one and the same thing. Worship is suddenly active and alive. It is swept up in life itself, more common to me than the chemistries of my own blood. Necessity and nature acting in full agreement one with the other.

All the connecting cords are bound together in the great bond of his love. To love the God who abides in my neighbor is impossible without loving my neighbor. I am bound to my neighbor by my love for God.

Again, the math is not all that difficult. This is not too deep or too obscure to understand. Nature is not deep. It is not obscure. It might be distracted. It might be overlooked or undervalued, but it is not outside understanding. It is too suffuse, too evident, too present around us, too immediate.

Man in God is man in love.

Love, therefore, is our transport, our fare to a living Eden. Love is paradise come again. Without a complete reckoning with love, there is no reconciliation with our origins. Man without God is man without love. Man without love is not fully man; selfhood is at best imaginary.

. . . .

The love of God is not merely something that can somehow profitably be fitted into a man's life. It is man's whole reason for existing, and until he loves God man does not really begin to live.

THOMAS MERTON
THE LAST OF THE FATHERS

. . . .

As I have come to understand the devoted life, that life that buys back my authenticity, that remembers my origins, that infuses the life of God into every action I take, however small or grand that action might be, I have come to appreciate Bernard even more. He was an inspired mix of severity and dazzle, of lightning and tenderness, revelation and plainsong.

. . . .

The believing soul longs and faints for God; she rests sweetly in the contemplation of him.

BERNARD OF CLAIRVAUX
ON LOVING GOD

. . . .

four degrees of love

Bernard says there are four degrees of love, four ascending steps that lead to union with God, union being at the height of our ascent.

* * * * * * * * * * * * * * * * * * *

*In the beginning man loves God, not
for God's sake, but for his own.*

BERNARD OF CLAIRVAUX
ON LOVING GOD

* * * * * * * * * * * * * * * * * * *

Man loves his master, yes, but in his initial flight from the world, his first inclination is to save himself. In his recognition of God, he indeed comes to love God, but it is still somewhat out of a concern for *self.* This progression is natural and good. This is the first degree of love.

But this initial taste only increases his deeper appetite for God, and from there man moves on to loving others and God, which, again, is right and good, but it is still for his, not God's, sake. This is the second degree of love. Man legitimately loves God, and now he loves others, but his love is still bound to *self.*

> Does such a life explain all the mysteries? Not at all. The mystery of God remains intact—beautiful, impenetrable, and above all, interesting.

In the third degree of love, man begins to love God for God's own sake. This is the stage where our surrender approaches completeness (remembering that surrender itself is from our origins). Indeed, Adam was surrendered completely to God, so much so that the word itself never came up. It was implied. Surrender was part of existence itself. It was written in foliage, in the air, in the water supply, even as it was imprinted on the heart of man. Surrender sweetened man's innocence, and more so by not having to mention its name.

In this stage, *self* loses its long-standing bid for sovereignty. We could even say that the very martyrdom love asks of us is realized in this transition. The necessary death:

> Whoever finds his life will lose it, and whoever loses his life
> for my sake will find it.
>
> —MATTHEW 10:39; SEE ALSO 16:25;
> MARK 8:35; LUKE 9:24; 17:33; JOHN 12:25

There is one more degree of love yet to attain: when man is able to love himself for God's sake alone. Here, union with God is realized. It is no less than a consummation, to employ God's own metaphor. *Self* is vanquished. It is absorbed, swept up in the life of God. Man can love himself because he loves God. It is the ultimate good, the ultimate rightness. He sees himself in God, a part of God. All distinctions between man and his master are lost. It is a delicious paradox posed by Bernard, for we are *lost* in God, yes, but we are *found* in him as well:

> For you died, and your life is now hidden with Christ in God.
> —COLOSSIANS 3:3

My relationship with my wife took a similar, though not exact, course. It simply proves that love is one thing and not another. Love is singular. It has one true mind, one way. Sure, it was love at first sight. But in those initial moments it was more about *my* sensation, the riot going on in *my* heart, the confusion in *my* senses. My heart, to say it mildly, was set on pilgrimage. Stage one.

The world around me took on a sudden glow. I began to love everything and everyone in it. But it was still the rapid movement in *my* blood, the overturning of *my* inner kingdom. Ah, stage two. Then, as it matured in me I began to see *her* more fully. *Self* was redirected. It began its recession out of the foreground. It became less and less about *me* and more about *her* at stage three.

By stage four, we were husband and wife. Consummation, legal union, the happy triune agreement between God, her, and me. She and I became one flesh. But am I confusing my own nuptial life with God's? I can only hope so. When I consider our 25 years, Bernard of Clairvaux seems as current as today's weather.

"turn back, dull earth, and find thy centre out"

Having said all that, not that terribly long ago I felt myself a stranger to love. As a poet, as a writer, I discovered that my words had plenty of lyric, but little life, it seemed. It had all the music, but it had somehow lost its heart. Or it felt that way to me. It happens. Either way, it was difficult to live with. I felt myself a stranger to God, and having been involved in full-time Christian service for 20 years or so, this was an unsettling place to find myself. My spirituality had become a matter of talk. Noise and talk. Wag.

My dogs loved me. They couldn't help themselves. It's what they do. They let me know it. It didn't matter to them how flawed I felt myself to be. The more I suffered, the harder they loved. Another reason for books like this.

I am not sure of the exact moment, and it is not important, but at some critical moment I understood clearly that I needed to find the center again. I had been thrown out of orbit. All my compass readings were off. As Romeo says in Juliet's orchard, his own private Eden, "Can I go forward when my heart is here? Turn back, dull earth, and find thy centre out."[4] That was me, the lovestruck, the afflicted. I strongly suspected my faith was out of center, that over the years perhaps it had fallen out of alignment, but at the moment I was cupid blind. *What to do? What to do?*

Though I had no such name for it at the time, I began my own *work of rediscovery* to find my way back, to regain the center I had lost. As I have already said, each one of us has such a work before us. Culture has grown more and more hostile to Christianity, more and more anti-Christ. There is a gathering uneasiness, a general droop in the landscape. The world is heating up, and at many levels. It is also getting more crowded. God has been cast out of this pseudo-paradise, and with him, love has been officially redefined and devalued.

> [Bernard] was an inspired mix of severity and dazzle, of lightning and tenderness, revelation and plainsong.

With so much noise, with all the image mongers, all the cultural prophets and profiteers demanding so much of us, any migration toward the center is hardly possible without severe rethinking and, perhaps, a bit of divine intervention.

The devoted life, as blithe, as casual, and with as gentle a spirit as this book defines it, is nonetheless of critical importance to each of us. For all its lightness, it is not to be taken lightly. Outside such a life there is only pretense, artifice, images, paintings of life, and more fiction. A dim half-life. If time has told us anything, the old formulas neither satisfy nor do they work, at least not for the serious or the desperate, remembering that the violent take it by force when necessary.[5]

But whatever I was to find on my search, I found it, and almost as quickly as I began. Now Bernard would say that the moment I began to search for that center, or that I began to search for God, was the very moment I had him, *all of him*, that I would not have begun such a search had God not desired to be sought and put the search in me to begin with. God is the one who initiates movement toward himself.

* *

But here is a paradox, that no one can seek the Lord
who has not already found Him. It is Thy will,
O God, to be found that Thou mayest be sought,
to be sought that Thou mayest the more truly be found.

BERNARD OF CLAIRVAUX
ON LOVING GOD

* *

No, this is not a spiritual Rubik's Cube, although it is a delicious piece of text, is it not? I have found this to be true many times. It seems that when I am desperate for God, he is more immediate somehow. And is any good romance ever without a touch of the desperate? When I consider that my prayers are inspired by God, that the words that form in my mouth are shaped by him, I begin to understand the living current that passes between us, that stage four is alive and fertile in me. He does not settle for partial possession. He longs for union. Eden without man is a lonely place.

I vowed that every day for an entire year I would write about love. If you asked where such a strategy came from, I could not tell you, at least not at the time. I could write as little or as much as I desired, and I could write whatever I wanted, with one condition: it had to be about love, and love alone. I would not allow myself to rise from my chair or quit until the entry was complete.

I had no thought of publication. This was too personal. This was a thing between God and me. It had the feel of a reckoning.

• • • • • • • • • • • • • • • • • • • •

My heart says of you, "Seek his face!"
Your face, Lord, I will seek.

PSALM 27:8

• • • • • • • • • • • • • • • • • • • •

I felt that once my own ideas ran dry, as I suspected they soon would, God would have to educate me, mentor me, father to child, and show me not only what I had missed but also what I had refused to even imagine about love.

I knew some things about love. I wasn't totally bereft. After all, I had a successful marriage. I had a wife who loved God. I had two great sons. I had three great dogs. I wrote and sang songs about loving God and loving my neighbor. I was an indefatigable journal keeper, and many of my pages were drippy with love. Yet I suspected it was a sham, or that much of it was, that all my talk was just that, talk, wag, that all my nice speeches were just more idiot commentary.

So I plunged in, all desire and blindness, reckless craving. I did not think about the consequences. I wasn't sure what to think. Desperation clears the mind of debris, strips it down to essentials. Desperation is a powerful charm between God and man.

a touch of the desperate

Since the word "desperate" has come up, it is worth a slight detour. It is a useful word. It has nice poetic weight and makes a great lyric. It carries a lot of presence in our songs and in our texts. We love the way it sounds in our prayers, and it preaches hot. Only I am not sure we actually have a living understanding of the word.

To be desperate is to act or feel against hope, to be bereft of hope. It is to be "driven to desperation, reckless or infuriated from despair. Hence, having the character of one in this condition; extremely reckless or violent, ready to run any risk or go any length."[6]

To be desperate in love is for desire to outweigh consequence. It is to be acutely aware of the absence—that living absence that has an almost physical texture—the void, that middle place in each of us that can only be filled or satisfied by the beloved. It is the great prioritizer. It is a sickness of heart, a sharp pain of appetite.

In corporate worship, it means that the song itself is immaterial; the music, the words, both lose meaning altogether. It is only the migration of the heart, the great movement toward God that matters. Upon this stream, this current, I lose myself completely, adrift, as I am, toward him.

Bernard observed a continual fast, imposing a type of desperation on his own body. His taste buds were so ruined he could hardly tell if he was drinking lamp oil or water. He had become the feast himself.

Getting back to my vow: I was too dumb to know the actual risks, but I thought it only right that if I were going to talk about love as much as I did, I should have a truer, more grownup knowledge of it. I knew, or at least I suspected, that God would intervene, that he and I would have school.

He did intervene, and quickly too, just like Bernard said. I began to listen as if for the first time. As I did, everything began to change. My first love was suddenly my first love again. Looking back, had I known the consequences, had I known the severity of love, the sweet violence in its heart, I would still have taken the risk.

> Desperation is a powerful charm between God and man.

If God were hungry, then like Bernard, I am become bread.

It was so simple, so plain before me. I felt like an even bigger idiot. My faith had been about so many other things. Love, yes, or maybe, well, kind of, but only an elementary understanding of it, some created half-love that is no love at all, an imagined likeness, an adolescent love, more a painting of love than real love.

For me, it was not unlike the deep arousal of love we read about in *White Fang*, the grand awakening, the inarticulate becoming articulate, having been wooed by the kindness of his master, the God who longed not to be feared so much as to be loved.

> Something, an incommunicable vastness of feeling, rose up
> into his eyes as a light and shone forth...the return of the
> love-master was enough. Life was flowing through him again,
> splendid and indomitable.
>
> —JACK LONDON, *WHITE FANG*

I made good on my vow, though much of it was the most awful unpublishable stuff you could ever read. Hyperbole, excess, mangled poetry, overstatement, drool, rant, repetition, and the near-clever curiosities that looked more like train wrecks than they did metaphors. But it had plenty of heart and the occasional moment of clarity, of something pure and unspoiled. At the end of 15 months I had a manuscript that was eight inches deep.

This had a twin effect. Not only did I make good on a vow, not only did I have my day of reckoning, my day of understanding, the grand awakening, when stage three gives way to stage four, but also, unknowingly, unconsciously perhaps, and by a design far outside my own power, it made a disciplined writer out of me. God proved himself, made himself large and conspicuous on my behalf. When love intervenes and makes what claim it comes to make, you are never the same again.

The result was eventually translated into print. After months of editorial savagery, it was done. I gave it the only name I could, that reduced the entirety of those 15 months into a simple lyric: *To Love Is Christ*, the book that read me, that echoes in these pages.

> God is the one who
> initiates movement
> toward himself.

By the way, Savannah was always at my feet. Quiet, warm, lovely. She never left my side however many hours I needed to spin it all out. That was years ago, and yet the metaphor that drives this book was between her and me the whole time. At the end of each session we took long walks. We were in West Virginia at the time, in Charleston, a river town, so we walked for hours by the water, every day, alone, together. It was a happy time.

So if I ask you to tell me about your faith, speak to me in the simplest terms you have. Do not give me cant or camp song. Do not give me your theology or other toys of thought. Just tell me how many fathoms deep you are in love.

● ● ● ● ● ● ● ● ● ● ● ● ● ● ● ● ● ● ●

Love is sufficient of itself; it pleases of itself, and for its own sake. It counts as merit to itself and is its own reward. Besides itself love requires no motive and seeks no fruit. Its fruit is its enjoyment of itself. I love because I love, and I love for the sake of loving. A great thing is love, if yet it returns to its Principle, if it is restored to its Origin, if it finds its way back again to its Fountainhead, so that it may be thus enabled to continue flowing with an unfailing stream. Amongst all the emotions, sentiments, and feelings of the soul, love stands distinguished in this respect, that in this one case alone has the creature the power to correspond and to make a return to the Creator in kind, though not in equality.

BERNARD OF CLAIRVAUX
SERMON 83, CANTICLE OF CANTICLES

● ● ● ● ● ● ● ● ● ● ● ● ● ● ● ● ● ●

● ● ● ● ● ● ●   a prayer of divine love   ● ● ● ● ● ● ● ●

If only I could love as my origins ask of me—purely, nakedly, thoroughly, correctly, naturally. If only the life of God in me were that fertile, that profuse, that liberal, that bounding, that alive in me, that irresistible. Yet I know Eden is but one kindness from me, one act of charity within my reach, one short surrender. Mine for the having. What violent a love must win you back! You are this riot in my blood, this confusion in my breathing. And may this bright creation, this big, round world you shaped with love in mind, giving it light and heat with a few select words, giving it a heart and a pulse, this ball of Earth that suspends like no other amid the planets and other orbiting things, that cries out even now in psalm before you, may my heart, like yours, break over it, and in the weeping find that joy that will sustain me. "Jesus, the very thought of thee."

In Christ, the life of God in me, Christ, him who gave me the right to say I'm in love. Amen.

*May love restore the innocence that
made it easy to believe.*

oh, how the world doth wag

When our life feeds on unreality, it must starve.

THOMAS MERTON
THOUGHTS IN SOLITUDE

Blow up your TV, throw away the paper
Move to the country, build you a home
Plant a little garden, eat a lot of peaches
Try to find Jesus, on your own.

JOHN PRINE
"SPANISH PIPE DREAM," JOHN PRINE

It's part fantasy, part community, and I can pay my bills naked.

MUST LOVE DOGS,
COMMENT ABOUT THE INTERNET
SCREENPLAY BY GARY DAVID GOLDBERG
BOOK BY CLAIRE COOKE

THE ONE THING I ALWAYS APPRECIATED about my dogs was the silence. In my study, for instance, once they had settled in, whether it was one, two, or all three of them, once the initial excitement of just being there had dissipated, once the work of resettling was done, all the little circles and all other decisions were made, they became very still. I knew they were there. I knew they were close to me. But other than a long sigh now and then, the slight jingle of a collar, a shuffle, rolling over, or the sound of breathing which I could barely hear anyway, there was no sound. Engaged as I always was in some project, it was not difficult to take their silence for granted, even as appreciative as I was of it.

It could be that way for hours. No movement. No sound. They knew I was close, and that was pill enough for what appeared to be undisturbed sleep. There were times I stopped what I was doing to see if they were still there. The stillness for a creature so otherwise alive and animated amazed me—how deep the contentment, and how refreshing it must be, once I thought about it, not to *have* to say anything. Another reason to envy the dog.

> How can you not love such creatures? How can you not love an animal whose greatest joy is being with the one she loves the most? That, and sticking her head out the window. I think eternity will be like that.

Dogs default to silence. Though not fixed, it is nonetheless their normal state. They don't seem to have to work at it as hard as we do. They are at home with silence. They do not fear it. Maybe it has to do with the long, vigilant hours the hunt demanded of them in their distant past—the stalking, the watch they kept in perfect stillness. Though I admit it is difficult to think that the coyote and the wolf are of the same genetic stripe as the Maltese or the shih tzu. A pack of shih tzu lying in wait is too much to imagine. Either way, when God thought these creatures up, he thought it best for them so he gave them a high tolerance for silence, as well as a tolerance for long stretches of solitude. All the wag is behind them.

For you and me, however, he seemed to leave that one out.

No, they were not silent all the time. With three dogs, riot could break out any minute, and one had to be prepared. The need for engagement was too strong, too much of a temptation, and all three of them pegged me for a sucker. And I was. Still am. *Dog's best friend*, that's me. I think it has something to do with the generosity of their spirit, their immediate delight to accept you and for you to be pleased with them. How can you not love such creatures? How can you not love an animal whose greatest joy is being with the one she loves the most? That, and sticking her head out the window. I think eternity will be like that.

respect the mystery

Among the best of dogs—quiet dogs, yappy small dogs, privileged dogs, nervous dogs, good-natured dogs, big lazy dogs—if there really is a silence-is-a-good-thing rule, there are also exceptions. Of course there are. With living things you have to make room for exceptions.

I was working with my son Adam last summer. He has an organic pest control company in Tennessee. Business was good. His workload was increasing, and he asked me to come along and help. One of the houses he serviced had an Akita in the backyard. The Akita is a Japanese dog, a very serious-minded, no-nonsense kind of dog—things I learned later. At the time, I knew nothing of the breed. It was a dog. I knew that. All dogs are alike, right? So I took the immediate posture of well-meaning-nice-guy-getting-the-confidence-of-the-animal-because-I-am-good-at-this, I-know-what-I'm-doing, I-wrote-the-book, dogs-love-me. Truth is, I doubt seriously if I had any such thought whatsoever.

As the dog approached the fence, which he did slowly, circumspectly, without thinking about what I was doing I reached in to pet him. Mistake. And an immediate "stupid, stupid, stupid" detonated in my head. I still have the scar on my right index finger as a reminder. I am glad to have that finger at all. I would not be able to point without it, play my guitar the same again, or hit a clean J on my computer keyboard. It was a very short skirmish, but a decisive one. Akita 1, David 0.

Having a good time with my son, and eager to get the work going, I'd gotten out of the car and was at the fence before Adam had any time to warn me: "Oh yeah, don't try to pet the dog. Says right here." But I wasn't upset with the animal. How could I be? It wasn't that he was mean. I was dumb. True to his breed, to his own conscience, true to the law in his blood, he was just being himself. I paid no attention to the rules of engagement, those natural laws of predation, aggression, submission, dominance, and so on. I just charged in. The bite was deep, and it took quite a while for the bleeding to stop. But it was a lesson learned. *I will respect the mystery. I will observe the rules of engagement.*

The Akita, whose name I never got, made no sound whatsoever. I approached the dog with a kind of idiot confidence. He didn't bark. He didn't growl. His actions said nothing to me (as if it would have mattered). He gave nothing away. There was nothing in his movement that said danger. He walked slowly toward me, confidently, with a kind of nobility in his step, and I, in good faith, offered the right hand of fellowship. *Stupid, stupid, stupid.*

the quiet heart

Perhaps I do not need to make the argument for how valuable silence is to the devoted life, how necessary a quiet heart is for anyone who seeks communion with God, who wishes to meet with him in private, beneath the surfaces of life. He is a very present God, as close or closer than your next breath. He is also a God of heights and depths, an omnipresent God who stands at some remove from us, a distance apart, as remote as the universe is wide.

He is extreme *other*, and yet he loves me and desires nothing more than my company. How am I to resolve such a paradox? For he has not told me everything. Nor is he obligated to tell me everything. I am therefore awestruck. I live just outside explanation. I live with wonder, and I am a friend to God. This is the odd condition, the strange love sickness of the devoted life.

I have learned the lesson I have been taught. I will respect the mystery. I will observe the rules of engagement.

The interesting thing about God is that, yes, to come to him with a quiet heart is not only acceptable but preferred. But if I had to wait for my heart to quiet itself to come to God, I would never come to God. God would be very lonely. A quiet heart is a heart under command, a heart under government or rule—things that cannot be said of the unquiet heart.

The unquiet heart is the heart that has become its own Judas, its own Absalom, an ungoverned heart, a renegade heart that has become its own master. I have more than 200 journals of unquiet heart on my shelves. My songs are a monument to unquiet heart. Mine is a soul in need of government, in need of a master. While I admit that need to be a great one, I also realize I am not alone.

• • • • • • • • • • • • • • • • • • •

As the deer pants for streams of water,
so my soul pants for you, O God.

My soul thirsts for God, for the living God.
When can I go and meet with God?
My tears have been my food day and night,
while men say to me all day long,
"Where is your God?"
These things I remember as I pour out my soul:
how I used to go with the multitude,
leading the procession to the house of God,
with shouts of joy and thanksgiving among
the festive throng.
Why are you downcast, O my soul?
Why so disturbed within me?
Put your hope in God,
for I will yet praise him,
my Savior and my God.
My soul is downcast within me;
therefore I will remember you
from the land of the Jordan,
the heights of Hermon—from Mount Mizar.
Deep calls to deep
in the roar of your waterfalls;
all your waves and breakers
have swept over me.
By day the LORD directs his love,
at night his song is with me—
a prayer to the God of my life.

PSALM 42:1-8

• •

The good news is this (and there is always good news): If you do not have a quiet heart, he will give you one. He makes his available for the asking:

The LORD your God is with you, he is mighty to save. He will take great delight in you, he will quiet you with his love, he will rejoice over you with singing.

—ZEPHANIAH 3:17

It is the master's voice, the one I recognize above all others in the midst of all my noise—comforting, quieting, assuring. The recognition itself is sweet, sufficient.

the call of a deeper appetite

Even Jesus needed an escape to a quiet place now and then. It was a necessity even for him, for the Son of God himself. And it wasn't just because great crowds followed him that he needed a break. *Jesus do this. Jesus do that. My son is deaf. My wife is blind.* No, his reasons were higher than that, and it had everything to do with private communion with his father, that dialogue between him and his master. It was like breathing or food. Sustenance. It was the call of a deeper appetite.

> Very early in the morning, while it was still dark, Jesus got up, left the house and went off to a solitary place, where he prayed.
> —MARK 1:35

Most of us have little clue how to quiet ourselves, if we think it necessary at all. There are those of us who are drawn to solitude or quiet, and those who see little point in it, those who are indifferent, and those who go to great lengths to avoid it. I am afraid I am of the former. As rare as it is, I like solitude. When I was a kid, we moved around a lot, and as difficult as it was at times, I had to learn how to be alone. At times I think I learned too well. But it shaped me and made me who I am. Writing demands a lot of solitude, and my gravitation toward the craft was a natural response to life.

But I also love the company of others. I have come to love the sound of the human voice, even in simple conversation. There is music in it if you listen and know what to listen for. When two or more voices join together, even in the simplest exchange, there is a kind of harmony to it that is nice, a polyphony that is pleasing to the heart. I am convinced that this is one of the more agreeable rewards of the devoted life—not only to find beauty where you wouldn't think to look for it but to recognize that a kind of poetry exists, a poetry of divine authorship, a psalmody that rises and sings in the midst of us.

These small glimpses of paradise awaken my desire, bring it right up front, put a sudden dryness in my mouth, a thirst for a higher life. And it is only right that we hunger for it, that each of us suffers at least some small pang of homesickness. Eden is the voice beneath all our collected voices, that faint lyric I hear, that sweetness that has no explanation.

Because it is so faint, so elusive, quiet becomes important to me. This particular quiet does not mean the exclusion of all noise. In this age, that might be too much to ask. No, there is a quiet we may enjoy in the midst of all the noise: the quiet center.

Quiet is a condition of the heart.

In the context of an acquiring God, a God who seeks us with a sweetness and a severity we can hardly understand, a God who is willing to be sought by us, quiet is a good thing. Solitude is a necessity at times. It is not exile. It is not banishment. On the contrary, it is a response to the God who ordains it, who says to come inside and sit for a while, "I long for your company." His voice is sweet to me. The voice of home, the voice of my deep memory, the voice of my origins.

In a driven age, any instruction toward quiet almost seems counter to popular culture or even popular theology. It seems too grave, too severe. It is not attractive. There is very little conspicuous *wow* value in deliberate quiet.

Culture, after all, is about community—or at least the image of community, about exchange and the noise of human commerce. It is a bustling marketplace, and a Christianity that mingles with popular culture should be anything but sedate, tranquil, or at rest. Indeed, the world must look toward a dynamic, moving, politically engaged though correct, kinetically wired, morally flexible, culturally aware, animated body of believers. Or at least this is the myth we feed upon.

Psalm 131 is much more than just a nice arrangement of words or a record of groans. Considering the author, more than likely the knowledge was hard earned, as was the clarity in his words. You might even detect a slight deflation in the tone, as joy might sound after a struggle, something this psalmist understands. Yet his optimism is as large as his God, bound as that optimism is in the calming of his soul. In a prayer of humility, of awareness, obligation, trust, and ultimately of hope, he affirms:

My heart is not proud, O LORD, my eyes are not haughty; I do not concern myself with great matters or things too wonderful for me. But I have stilled and quieted my soul; like a weaned child with its mother, like a weaned child is my soul within me. O Israel, put your hope in the LORD both now and forevermore.

—PSALM 131:1-3, A SONG OF ASCENTS, OF DAVID

Most of us are not convinced that quietude is a necessary element of the devoted life. Our actions say this. We leave these things to the mystics, to the Mother Teresas and Francis of Assisis, the Brother Lawrences, the Bernards, the people we read about and perhaps admire greatly but who lived in a world far removed from our own—a world before television and iPods, a technobarren world, men and women who wore cowls and sackcloth, who loved their poverty and chose it willingly as their gift to God.

On the contrary, Scripture invites us to become intimate with silence, to befriend it, even as it is a friend to us, a generous friend at that, one who serves us with great benefit. There are many instances in Scripture where Jesus calmed loud and boisterous things, whether it was a raging sea or a man gone out of his senses.[1] A word or two was sufficient:

"Peace, be still!"

MARK 4:39 NKJV

The silence of God is fertile, revelatory, prolific, redemptive, filled utterly with himself. All this, and still the hush is profound, bottomless, like his love.

prepare to meet your God

I have always imagined Elijah as a solitary creature, a loner. After all, he did notorious things: large, daring, outrageous things that set him apart from most any other personality in Scripture. It is not so easy, however, to picture him being quiet. But if you look closer, he embraced it. He pursued quiet as he pursued most everything else—with an almost savage aggression. And "savage" is not a bad way to describe Elijah's resolve. He would ask nothing less of himself. Is he extreme? Can we imagine him any other way? We love him for it.

The quiet he demanded of himself was just as extreme, just as savage.

The life of a prophet is a solitary one on many levels, by necessity, and for many reasons. For one, not everybody liked them, particularly evil kings and queens. Prophets were not very political, and they cared very little for small talk.[2] And because Elijah had slain 400 prophets of Baal, there was a serious amount of chafe between him and Jezebel.[3] (Now there is a name I might give a cat but *never* a dog. Jezebel is not a dog's name. Anyone who understands dogs knows what I mean.) Anyway, Jezebel swore to kill Elijah, and he took her seriously—so much so that he literally "ran for his life."[4]

Some things I will never understand in Scripture, and this is one of them. Here is a prophet of God, a man of severe confidence and command, a prototype of John the Baptist, and yet he is afraid of this painted woman, this demented queen.

Elijah's flight takes him all the way to Horeb, the mountain of God, not a short distance away. He stops in the desert long enough to eat, and then on the strength of that one meal, runs for the next 40 days and nights to hole up in a cave.

The Word of the Lord comes to Elijah and asks basically what he is up to. Something you might ask a friend: *"What are you doing here, Elijah?"* I am not sure we can make a Sunday school lesson out of this. Other than the large personalities involved, there is really nothing profound here to uncover. Elijah replies, "I have been very zealous for the LORD God Almighty. The Israelites have rejected your covenant, broken down your altars, and put your prophets to death with the sword. I am the only one left, and now they are trying to kill me too."[5]

Elijah is instructed to stand on the mountain in the presence of the Lord, because the Lord is about to pass by.

> Then a great and powerful wind tore the mountains apart
> and shattered the rocks before the LORD, but the LORD was
> not in the wind. After the wind there was an earthquake, but

the LORD was not in the earthquake. After the earthquake came a fire, but the LORD was not in the fire. And after the fire came a gentle whisper.

—1 KINGS 19:11-12

I love the New International Version of the Bible, but there are times when the King James does greater justice to a line. It says: "After the fire came a still small voice."

Whether you prefer a "gentle whisper" or "a still small voice," it is undeniably the voice of God. And as great as the Lord is, as majestic, as grand, as holy, he spoke to one of his own captains in the quiet hush of his mountain hold in the soft nothing of his voice.

Elijah had prepared himself to listen. His running, his fasting, the severity he imposed on himself, was not wildness as it might read to us. It was not manic flight. It was preparation, a quieting of his soul to listen to the voice of his master.

When desperation and wisdom meet and agree, they point us in the direction of God.

> And as great as the Lord is, as majestic, as grand, as holy, he spoke to one of his own captains in the quiet hush of his mountain hold, as it was expected, in the soft nothing of his voice.

There are commentaries with much more interpretive savvy than I am capable, teachers able to finesse meaning out of these passages with much more skill than I. For me, this particular lesson of Elijah is not one of *expectation*. With the show of violent nature—the wind, the earthquake, the fire—Elijah is not surprised. I am not convinced he learned anything new about hearing the voice of God or that he was reprimanded for mistakenly expecting to hear it in a larger, more conspicuous voice. Indeed, to call down fire upon the altar when he made sport with the prophets of Baal on Carmel or to cause the widow's cruse of oil to never run dry and her bins of flour to remain full, he would have had to hear quite clearly from God. He would have to know how it all works.

Characters like Elijah stand at such a distance from us, not only historically, but by the large stature of their names and their presence in Scripture. Elijah, Jacob, Moses. Even Paul, Peter, and John. It is easy to forget that these are still just men, men who for reasons known only to God were set apart. But men nonetheless, no different than the rest of us.

You and I have access to the same God, and in like manner we can hear his voice. Stories may never be told about us, songs may not be written, and no one may ever read about us in a book, but that doesn't mean it is any less real for you and me than it was for them. He is *the attainable God*, the *God of possibility*, and his desire to speak to you is greater than your desire to listen. Listening to God is a cooperation— one that He empowers.

Elijah was intimate with God. Intimacy itself is a type of quiet, a powerful one that frightens most of us. When the noise ceases between two individuals, when all the talk ends, when the veils are removed, there is only the other. It is a type of nakedness of which Elijah was not afraid.

> "Prepare to meet your God, O Israel." He who forms the mountains, creates the wind, and reveals his thoughts to man, he who turns dawn to darkness, and treads the high places of the earth—the LORD God Almighty is his name.
>
> **—AMOS 4:12-13**

Elijah is one of the more dominant people in the Bible, and yet we are denied much information about him. On the Mount of Transfiguration he is there with Moses and Jesus.[6] In Revelation 11, though not named directly, Bible scholars suspect Elijah will be one of the two "witnesses," again with Moses, who must prophesy for a number of days, and who the world must see before the end comes. Other than this, we have no record of Elijah's history.

He is from Tishbe, a town of disputed location, but somewhere in Gilead. He arrives in the book of 1 Kings *in medias res*, "in the midst of things." He is a seasoned, fully working prophet when we are introduced to him, arriving as from out of nowhere. Of course, if we look at the odd image the typical prophet makes, the way he dresses, the town he comes from, the obscurity stamped upon him, maybe even his eating habits, then "from out of nowhere" may be all we want to know about him. His story is all action, high drama. Action taken on the strength of a quiet heart.

Intimacy itself is a type of quiet, a powerful one that frightens most of us.

Elijah knew how to listen to God and what his voice sounded like. All the elements of Earth tried to convince him, and as wild as they were, as ominous and foreboding, he wasn't moved. His quiet was too complete, immovable, absolute. Like the dog, he knew his master's voice amid the clamor of other voices.

I don't see a look of surprise on Elijah's face. I see one of peace. He hasn't eaten for 40 days, not to mention the running. His body is hushed, his appetites are under management, and he has done all of this purposely. *He is at peace.* His quiet is a deep one, penetrable only by God. The elements have no power over him. As contrary as the reality is to the image, Elijah, the great prophet, the outrageous personality of the Old Testament, the cantankerous, quick-tempered, fireball-hurling, sack-clothed, bearded man of God is a man of quiet.

When desperation and wisdom meet and agree, they point us in the direction of God.

He loves to hear the voice of God. He loves it so much he has learned to command his own flesh, like Saint Bernard, perhaps a bit more severely than you and I are accustomed to, but nonetheless, it all has one center, one purpose, and that is to nurture the life between God and him, to keep the current alive, fluid, active, prolific, fertile, immediate. This *is* his life. He respects the mystery, and not only observes, but lives by the rules of engagement.

Stillness, calmness, tranquility, peacefulness. However you choose to describe it, such a state is possible only by way of relationship with the master. It is found in him alone. Quietness, according to Scripture, is the very thing God works in you, that he achieves in you. Why? Because his desire for union is greater than your own.

the threshing floor

The heart is a threshing floor where we are sifted, where God meets with us and instructs us and imposes his peace upon us.

> The fruit of righteousness will be peace; the effect of righteousness will be quietness and confidence forever.
> —ISAIAH 32:17

Quiet is not so foreign to us as we imagine. It was part of our original package. We were equipped with it from the beginning. For quiet was just as necessary then as it is now for listening to the voice of God. Eden is the garden of the quiet heart.

Adam suffered no distance between God and himself. There were no barriers, no obstacles. There was no noise, no wag, nothing anxious in his thoughts. Words were living things, and none of them were wasted. He did not labor, strive, or negotiate with his soul to communicate with God. The border between humanity and divinity was as thin as mist. Like Elijah, Adam's quiet was complete and thorough. It possessed all of him. There was hardly need to talk.

To regain the quiet heart is to regain paradise. Is it beyond our reach now? Is Eden so buried? Is the spot on the old map so lost, erased, or forgotten? Deep memory says *no*. The devoted life wakes the Eden sleeping in the midst of us.

Psalm 23 is the classic psalm of restfulness, tranquility, submission, nurture, confidence, mutual having, and leading. These elements combine with majesty in the music of the King James:

> The Lord is my shepherd; I shall not want.
> He maketh me to lie down in green pastures: he leadeth me beside the still waters.
> He restoreth my soul: he leadeth me in the paths of righteousness for his name's sake.
> Yea, though I walk through the valley of the shadow of death, I will fear no evil: for thou art with me; thy rod and thy staff they comfort me.
> Thou preparest a table before me in the presence of mine enemies: thou anointest my head with oil; my cup runneth over.

Surely goodness and mercy shall follow me all the days of my
life: and I will dwell in the house of the LORD for ever.

—PSALM 23:1-6

The quiet of God is anything but empty. It is as alive as his Word
is alive, as his Christ is alive. The quiet that David refers to in Psalm
131 and in Psalm 23 is a living quiet filled with the life of God. To
pursue this quiet is to pursue God—emptiness and fullness conflated
together, completing one another in the mystery of God. But even the
best of writers can only hope to awaken the appetite, to kindle desire.
We seek too fervently the quiet for ourselves.

amid all that blab

We seem to like our noise. No, we love it. We do not feel engaged with
life without it, like something is missing. The currents just outside our
little world are moving too fast and with too much sparkle. Being quiet
can be downright disturbing, creepy. Why? Because we are faced with
the insoluble riddle of being alone with ourselves.

Intimacy, even with ourselves, is a type of quiet, a nakedness that
often unsettles us. So we pursue noise, preferring it above the solace
of a quiet moment to ourselves. I am not sure we want to know the
reasons why. This is nothing new.

* * * * * * * * * * * * * * * * * * * *

O baffled, balk'd, bent to the very earth,
Oppress'd with myself that I have dared to open my mouth,
Aware now that amid all that blab whose echoes
recoil upon me I have not once had the least idea
who or what I am...

WALT WHITMAN
"AS I EBB'D WITH THE OCEAN OF LIFE,"
LEAVES OF GRASS

* * * * * * * * * * * * * * * * * * * *

We live in an age of swiftly moving, swiftly changing images, an
age of sensation and spectacle. We live in an age of elevated sound,

much of it artificial, an age of spin, of puff and wind, of loud voices and a lot of empty air. Sound dominates our spaces, fills all our gaps. And not only are we comfortable with it, we cannot seem to do without it or get enough of it.

We are saturated with noise. It is one of the more salient features of present culture. There are other names for it—names we wouldn't use in church perhaps, street names, less sanctified names. We can just call it *wag*. Both noun and verb, we are fed so much of it, so much empty talk, so much wind, so many opinions, we hardly know how to separate what is relevant, what is true, what is worth listening to, and what is not.

We are overcome with wag. We know it is empty. We just don't seem to care.

Realizing this almost a year ago, my wife and I took John Prine's advice, and though we did not actually blow up our TV, we did remove it from our lives. It was close enough to an act of violence. It was not a mere fast we called, a postponement or a moratorium. It was permanent. It was a simple modification of our life, but a significant one. It was a start.

Now, whenever the subject comes up, we find we do not miss television at all. The quiet at first was stark, conspicuous. In short time we realized just how rich and generous it is. Like something we truly missed. We reclaimed a part of our lives. We are not afraid of missing the news, of not knowing who wins what or who is the prince and who is the toad or Oprah's latest endorsement. All that glorious spin that drives culture about.

We discovered that this small change brought us one degree closer to each other. That alone was worth all the fuss. It is a subtle distinction, because we never watched that much television to begin with. My wife, like our dogs, was always rather indifferent to it. Our sons were not raised with the family TV always *on* like a favorite pet or a relative.

Conversation is a better pastime, as are books, and time with God, without the pressure of having to choose between him and another episode of *House*.

And there is always the small miracle of a walk.

With a poet's skill at observation, Walt Whitman brings back the large generous humanity of simple conversation:

> Loafe with me on the grass, loose the stop from your throat,
> Not words, not music or rhyme I want, not custom
>   or lecture, not even the best,
> Only the lull I like, the hum of your valved voice.[7]

—WALT WHITMAN, "SONG OF MYSELF,"
LEAVES OF GRASS

Like most families in the fifties and sixties, my brother and I were raised with television. It was still a novelty, part of the magic of the post-World War II optimism. At that time it was *Howdy Doody, Rin Tin Tin*, and of course, *Lassie*. My favorite cartoon characters were always dogs—*Huckleberry Hound, Augie Doggie and Doggie Daddy, Deputy Dawg, Precious Pup,* and *Mighty Manfred the Wonder Dog*. Boomers will remember these names with pride.

Today television babysits our kids, shares the responsibility of raising them. Part nanny, part noise, all of it artificial, teaching them the *whys* and *hows* of a consuming anti-Christ culture, feeding them a lot of pictures of food but no real food.

• • • • • • • • • • • • • • • • • • • •

If the doors of perception were cleansed everything
would appear to man as it is: Infinite.

WILLIAM BLAKE
THE MARRIAGE OF HEAVEN AND HELL

• • • • • • • • • • • • • • • • • • • •

Although my wife and I have given up television, I am not at all preaching that you must do the same. This was *our* strategy, *our* way to draw closer to the center again. After all, God put his life in specific places, and we simply decided to seek those places out and avoid the rest.

But however it affects us, and whatever decisions we have made about television or any of the toys of our techno-dependent culture, unreality is the enemy of the devoted life. Thomas Merton wrote wisely, "When our life feeds on unreality, it must starve."[8]

I say this as a caution only. We are a generation of feeders, of consumers, of insatiates feeding on imaginary food like Peter Pan and his Lost Boys. We are starving and we hardly know it because culture is too busy convincing us otherwise. The image glitters before us. It sparkles in our eyes. Who can resist that?

· · · · · · · · · · · **prayer of quiet** ▸ · · · · · · · · ·

Lord, I am a stranger to quiet, and therefore I am a stranger to myself. If I have missed you, if I have been caught in the traps of my own noise, if I have been charmed by the winds, if I have been moved by voices other than your own, it is the impostor I see in the mirror and not me at all. Having you, I have me. Show me where we can meet, you and I. Speak to me in the small hush of love, the voice Elijah heard at Horeb. I will not fear the silence you ask. I will submit my whole heart and persist stubbornly with every sinew of my strength because you are there in the quiet center, between the cherubim, the silent guard. Like the psalmist, I will quiet myself because that is what you ask. I want to enjoy your presence, to breathe your perfumes, to lose myself completely in the sweet delirium of paradise. I will not examine too closely things that are beyond me. I will trust you for my good.

In Christ, where God meets with me in quiet, Christ, the soft nothing of his voice. Amen.

May your soul be a resting place for God himself.
When the son of man has no place to lay his head,
may your heart be home enough.

6

if i love you,
who cares what time it is?

He has made everything beautiful in its time.
He has also set eternity in the hearts of men;
yet they cannot fathom what God has done
from beginning to end.

ECCLESIASTES 3:11

He said, "You work each day from 8 to 5,
And you wait for Friday to arrive,
You geniuses have got it wrong,
My weekend lasts a whole week long."

ALLEN LEVI, "TALKING WITH TYLER"
I'D RATHER BE A DOG THAN A DUDE LIKE YOU

TIME HAD NO JURISDICTION OVER THEM. It was something they had little use for. There were no deadlines to meet, and there was nowhere in particular to be. They honored no schedule other than the one we imposed on them. They had no concept of rush and hustle, no neurotic association with haste, except perhaps when it came to food, bounding out of the van, or if the doorbell rang. They were not concerned about what was happening later in the afternoon. Early and late did not exist. Life was something they did in the moment they were living it, not before, not after.

Everything was present tense. But that is a bit misleading because "present" implies a past and a future, and my dogs lacked any concern for either one. Other than the necessary link between time and instinct, those internal mechanisms of survival that engage the memory, time was a nonissue to them. It had no voice in the decisions they made.

- -

*I take my dogs to the same spot every day, yet
each day I'm amazed to see them act as if they are
in a new and magic land for the first time.*

JEFFREY MASSON
DOGS NEVER LIE ABOUT LOVE

- -

In spite of this aloofness to time, a dog's memory is still better than a human's. Some may argue this point. But if it is true, perhaps it is because you and I overburden our memories with emotional millstones. The processing is what makes the difference. Whatever the truth, a dog has the capability to engage fully in the moment, to give the moment all her attention. She is willing to invest all of herself to the moment because the moment is all that exists for her.

Because she pays no homage to time, the dog can draw from life its fullest measures, its boundless liberality and generosity, the things we deny ourselves. When she plays, she plays hard and completely. When she loves, she invests her entire being. In grief she holds back nothing. In her possession of the moment, the dog maintains a certain preparation for whatever happens, a readiness that renders time and its odd hypnosis mute.

For memory to work properly, there has to be some perception of time somewhere, some observance of its rule. Dogs will delight in people or animals they have known or have come to love even when separated by long stretches of time. In Homer's classic tale *The Odyssey*, Odysseus had been away from home for 20 years. On his return, his dog, Argos, now old, feeble, immobile, lying on a dung heap, full of fleas, uncared for but still alive, upon hearing his master's voice, recognizes him immediately. The dog doesn't have the strength to move toward him, but he wags his tail and lowers his ears in pure joy. Odysseus has to wipe a tear from his own face lest his identity be detected.[1] The dog then dies fulfilled and happy. (Between you and me, I suspect Homer had a dog.)

We have to have a past if we are to remember anything. Time is linear. It moves in a straight line. Past, present, and future can be plotted in a concrete and measurable order. A thing remembered is a thing that once was, an event capable of being catalogued and dated. There is a certain amount of reach backward.

For the dog, a past is expedient only as it helps trigger alarm or delight. This might be her only link to time itself. She is otherwise unaware of it. A dog will not likely repeat a behavior that has brought her harm. Memory, in this model, is a survival mechanism imbedded in instinct, more visceral than conscious.

You and I have a more complicated relationship with time than the dog does. Yesterday has little power over the dog. Dogs do not burden themselves with souvenirs, emotional or otherwise. This may explain their exceptional ability to forgive. After all, to remember an offense, you must have a past to keep it in. They have prodigious memory, but no past, at least not a past as you and I consider the past, a past that we approach with longing or regret, a past we weary ourselves either lamenting or celebrating in an attempt to rediscover meaning.

Because of this, and because a dog is not good with half measures, love has full access. Her devotion is sanitized. She can invest her full self into the worship experience. She is always present, always there.

like there is no tomorrow

Dogs actually live like there is no tomorrow. Life is reduced to a succession of clearly definable moments. This clarifies love for them and simplifies their faith. It defines the way they are able to love us. "I will give all to you *now* because *now* is what I have. *Now* is all I understand. *Now* has shaped my thought life and taught me how to love you." Past, present, and future are intangibles so the dog has little use for them. Everything is immediate, flush, present, and perhaps above all, relevant.

Nothing a dog does is arbitrary or frivolous, even in play. Every moment counts because the moment is all there is. She is able to love like there is no tomorrow because she has no tomorrow. It is not a cliché to the dog.

Now is more than just the immediate, more than the mere absence of chronological placeholders. We could say that *now* is the present, the immediate, but more. It is the present without the burden of a clock, the immediate with something a little extra, the present with none of the usual distractions, psychological and otherwise, of time.

Now is the exclusion of the linear restraints of time. Therefore, we can say that *now* exists just outside of time. But what does that mean? It means that we are not going to arrive at a satisfying definition of *now*. Explanation and understanding are inapplicable. It is a knowing of a different kind, of which the dog is wise, and perhaps the small child.

> Nothing a dog does is arbitrary or frivolous, even in play. Every moment counts because the moment is all there is. She is able to love like there is no tomorrow because she has no tomorrow. It is not a cliché to the dog.

Our psychology is bound to time in such a way that makes understanding of eternity or anything like eternity rather difficult. Difficult but not impossible. You and I have the capacity. Made in the likeness of God, we are the exception among all other life forms. We may not be aware of it, it might be sleeping somewhere or hidden beneath some emotional or spiritual debris, but we were given the capacity to understand eternity when we took our first breath.

Man was made to live in paradise. You and I were never meant to be strangers to eternity or to an understanding of it. But for whatever the reason, conditions exist that frustrate our awareness of things outside of time. For now, we must engage faith.

The dog doesn't have to try so hard. Time is not insufferably linked to her psychology as it is to ours. *Now* is easy. Believing is easy. She doesn't worry about *understanding* life; she is too busy living it.

The immediacy of *now* is intrusive, meddlesome. *Now* makes demands of you and me that cannot be diverted or put off. Of course, my dogs thought nothing of these things. Because time had no sovereignty in their thought life, their priorities were clear and easily managed.

When the end came for each of them, they didn't know they were old dogs. As it was with Argos, love was never old or tired. It was always eager. Other than a certain stiffness in the joints, a deceleration, a groan that is weaker, longer, lazier, a dog is not aware that she is aging.

he loved with a single heart

She had only one master, as it is said a dog must. It was also clear that Savannah loved her master—that is me, more than she loved herself. She seemed indifferent to my shortcomings. For her they didn't exist. If anyone had the goods on me, it was my dog. She heard every word, private and public, the delicate and the not so delicate. She was privy to every act, to all my rant and squall. She was unmoved by any of it. Nothing I did seemed to shock her or change her resolve toward me. Though the surface might be smeared with grime, she gave it little thought, having eyes for something finer just below it. Always adventurous, love approaches the heart of its beloved as if it were the last remaining frontier.

In his book *White Fang*, Jack London says his canine hero "loved with single heart." The creature's love for his master was liberated of all uncertainty. His heart was sure. His gaze was fixed. His focus clear and unclouded. His life was irrevocably joined to the great object of his love.

Sober, tenacious, indomitable, this singleness of heart gives devotion its immutable resolve. It authenticates worship, particularly as it applies to life. It puts the absolutes where they belong—back into our thought life, back into our relationships, back into our communities where they are most needed, back into culture where they languish at present for want of use.

In ancient times, Judaism was unique among all the religions of the world because of its insistence on the one God. Other religions had their multiple deities; Israel had its one. This is how God chose to be defined, then and now—in singleness.

> Hear, O Israel: The LORD our God, the LORD is one.
>
> —DEUTERONOMY 6:4

The image that represents God's relationship to his people, evident throughout Scripture, is that of a bride and bridegroom. This is the mystery that holds all of Scripture together. "This is now bone of my bones," the man said, "flesh of my flesh,"[2] which is to say, "This is now *essence of my essence*." There is no greater unity than this. It is the first of all communities—that which joins God and man.

Redemption implies singleness of heart, a peace with God made possible in Christ. Peace itself being a completeness, a reconciliation with our origins, a bringing together of separated parts—wholeness:

> In Christ Jesus you who once were far away have been brought near through the blood of Christ. For he himself is our peace, who has made the two one and has destroyed the barrier, the dividing wall of hostility, by abolishing in his flesh the law with its commandments and regulations. His purpose was to create in himself one new man out of the two, thus making peace, and in this one body to reconcile both of them to God through the cross, by which he put to death their hostility.
>
> —EPHESIANS 2:13-16

Because God knows us as he does, and because his concern for us is the concern of a loving father, a father who, above all fathers, truly knows what is best, it follows that singleness of heart is indeed *best* for us, that it is necessary if man is to live as he was designed to live, and at the highest possible level of his existence.

> The light of the body is the eye: if therefore thine eye be single, thy whole body shall be full of light. But if thine eye be evil, thy whole body shall be full of darkness. If therefore the light that is in thee be darkness, how great is that darkness! No man can serve two masters: for either he will hate the one, and love the other; or else he will hold to the one, and despise the other. Ye cannot serve God and mammon.
>
> —MATTHEW 6:22-24 KJV

To add another degree of severity, here is another way to say it: *If I give but a little, I give nothing at all.* Commitment to a master is an all-or-nothing proposition. The dog knows this whether you and I do or not. It is the lesson of the widow's mite. "Out of her poverty," Scripture says, she "put in *all* she had to live on."[3]

> Always adventurous, love approaches the heart of its beloved as if it were the last remaining frontier.

For my allegiance to be anything but a fiction, or worse, a deception, it must be given with a whole heart—all of it, with a touch of the absolute, that measure of divinity we may engage with God's blessing, a part of himself he is willing to share, which simply means that I must, as the hymn says, "surrender all."

In love and in faith there is neither alternative nor argument. "Though He slay me," Job says, "yet will I trust Him."[4] *That* is singularity. Never shy, James speaks up concerning good spiritual hygiene:

> Come near to God and he will come near to you. Wash your hands, you sinners, and purify your hearts, you double-minded.
>
> —JAMES 4:8

tyranny of the urgent

Unfortunately for most of us, one master just doesn't seem enough. Like the pagans, we seem to be under the spell of multiple gods and masters. Indeed, there are many of them competing for our servitude: money, fame, more money, sex, debt. Included in this pantheon is *time.*

Time can be a cruel master. In 1967, Charles Hummel gave it a name. He coined the phrase "tyranny of the urgent." He suggested that we forfeit our peace to "pressing" things and, in turn, in our dependency on time and our independency from God we forfeit a full and satisfying life. Hummel said the way to defend against this over-lordship is to live in absolute dependence on God. The benefits are conspicuous:

> Man is never so truly and fully personal as when he is living
> in complete dependence upon God. This is how personality
> comes into its own. This is humanity at its most personal.
>
> —CHARLES HUMMEL, *TYRANNY OF THE URGENT*

The most human we can be, therefore, is to live by our original blue-print, for the creature to live in absolute agreement with the Creator. The highest form our humanity can take is also its first. Our identity is clarified in our union with God. It is hidden in him.[5]

> My purpose is that [believers] may be encouraged in heart
> and united in love, so that they may have the full riches of
> complete understanding, in order that they may know the
> mystery of God, namely, Christ, in whom are hidden all the
> treasures of wisdom and knowledge.
>
> —COLOSSIANS 2:2-3

The devoted life is a defense against slavery, whether it be slavery to time or to any powers of this world. I am neither prey nor victim. Like the dog, in singleness of heart I can give the entirety of my life over to one master.

If *now* bears a likeness to eternity, and I suspect it does, my dogs thought little of it. If they couldn't sniff it, chase it, eat it, play with it, chew on it, growl at it, lick, love, or bury it, they had little use for it. Eternity was just not an issue to my dogs. It was one less thing they had to worry themselves about. Besides, it was too much like the life they were already enjoying.

· · · · · · · · · · · · · · · · · ·

Thou shalt have no other gods before me.

EXODUS 20:3 KJV

· · · · · · · · · · · · · · · · · ·

They had one god—me. They had access to that god and all the benefits of relationship with that god. They were not afraid to give themselves fully to that god, and they did not do it because I asked them. Nor did they do it because of my provision. They did it because devotion demanded it of them in observance of the Exodus 20:3 written in their blood. They loved because that is what they do.

They were not afraid to love completely, and they got the return they never asked for. Their god loved them openly. Their god enjoyed spending time with them, whether engaged in some activity or just doing nothing in each other's company. Doing nothing was as much fun as anything else. They didn't care. Immediacy and presence ruled in this paradise.

bearded old men

Time was their toy. They also had a habit of looking through a person and revealing what was in the heart. Though the same could be said of our dogs, I am referring to the Old Testament prophets. They were not very popular. They were often stoned, impaled, or thrown into pits. Prophets were rather annoying. Ask Ahab. "Oh, great, here comes trouble again. What now? Famine? Pestilence? My firstborn? Annihilation?"[6]

(By the way, Ahab's wife, Jezebel, got her comeuppance. I won't go into detail but dogs were involved. And a meal.)[7]

But the prophetic is not limited to bearded old men foretelling the future, then or now.[8] It is much larger than that. Those same men would be the first to agree. The prophetic life is the participation in the immediate and present life of God. It distills downward not only into words, but into the general flow of life itself. This is perhaps the main reason the devoted life is such a powerful life. If we say that life itself can take on the nature of a prayer, it is the prophetic—this touch of God—that makes it possible.

The agreement between God and you is a living agreement. It is alive and active, even as the Word of God is.[9] A simple act of kindness offered in love has as much prophetic life, as much living substance, covers as much distance as the words of Jeremiah. Life becomes inspired in an all-new and all-encompassing way. That simple act does not die or drift into forgetfulness, but remains alive generation to generation, one link to the next, leaving traces of itself in the most remote places, crossing natural barriers of time and space to get there.

A gentle kiss of fellowship has the life of God in it—life that is truly life. A cup of cold water offered in love or that anonymous bit of cash that somehow finds its way to the struggling single mother—these actions have prophetic life. They share the life of God. They live beyond themselves and bestow a certain mysticism upon ordinary life.

God lives, and you and I have been appointed to share his life. And in sharing the life of God, our actions, our inaction, our words, our meditations, every isolated act, every random act of charity, every casual word, our worship—our devoted life—all these things are alive as he is alive.

This excites me! The common courses of my day run rich with prophetic life. When I offer some kindness, however large or small, or when I sing with all the gratitude in my heart, both are alive with God. Life and worship become indistinguishable.

When I bring coffee to my wife in the morning as she rises and sweeten it with words of love or say a "little prayer," as she likes to call it, in that humble act I am participating in the life of God. And as small as it might seem, that act has life beyond the moment, life that reaches into the day before me. Not only that, but it sets unity in motion, which empowers me.

God wants us to enjoy our faith, to be at home with him, to love without thought or deliberation, for love and life to so join that each act has the stamp of deity on it. Anyone who loves God, anyone who participates in the life of God, operates in the prophetic—the living currency, the fluid life of God, that bit of him that mingles generously with our humanity, that sanctifies the temporal, making it holy and alive. And because eternity does not concern itself with proportion or dimension, the smaller, hidden, or even invisible acts have just as much life, just as much a share of divinity as larger ones.

Visiting the infirm, spending time with the aging widower, giving someone your full attention simply because they ask it of you, listening intently to their story, surrendering completely to the moment, the large kindness of remembering someone's name—as simple as these acts are, they are alive with God.

* *

Worship God! For the testimony of Jesus is the spirit of prophecy.

REVELATION 19:10

* * * * * * * * * * * * * * * * * * * *

to err is human, to forgive is all dog

Dogs are able to forgive with an ease you and I are incapable of. Perhaps time—or rather their indifference to time—has something to do with it. To forget requires time, linear, sequential time, which has no influence, no power over dogs. If I have no past, where am I to list all the offenses against me? Where is the record to be kept?

There could be other explanations. The dog's ability to forgive may be due simply to her outrageous capacity to love. Perhaps love has such sovereignty over her that it suffers no obstacle. Unforgiveness is an obstacle. It is a stone in the shoe of love.

When we live in the immediate, in the wonder of *now,* in that paradise present, we remove the venom from the past. It no longer has a voice within us. Love remains sovereign, making forgiveness much lighter work.

God forgives completely. One reason is that he gives himself no past to look back on. Time is less of an issue for God than it is for the dog. His sea of forgetfulness is a vast one. I do not understand it, and though I do not question it (that much), it nonetheless amazes me how an omnipotent, omniscient, omnipresent God can allow himself to forget. But this is his choice.[10] In his great love, he has given himself no option. Unforgiveness is incompatible with love.

You and I are not so fortunate. We build memorials to time—real ones and imaginary ones. We labor long and hard to ensure their durability, their resilience to the elements. We tend to keep long and detailed records of offenses. Unlike the dogs, and unlike God, we have a past to store them in and we call them up at will. Some of us, if not most of us, go so far as to find strange comfort in them. This is an odd psychology the dog doesn't suffer. For you and me, though time is linear, memory unfortunately is not.

How liberating it would be to forget. How redemptive. How much easier life would be if I were not haunted by the meddling and unkind ghosts of my past. These lines from Shakespeare's *Macbeth* were too good to pass over. Macbeth is seeking help from his doctor because Lady Macbeth is troubled:

> Canst thou not minister to a mind diseased,
> Pluck from the memory a rooted sorrow,

Raze out the written troubles of the brain
And with some sweet oblivious antidote
Cleanse the oppress'd bosom of that perilous stuff
Which weighs upon the heart?

—WILLIAM SHAKESPEARE, *MACBETH*

Other than the eloquence, this could easily be one of my prayers. *"Pluck from the memory a rooted sorrow."* Wicked king or not, fiction or nonfiction, Macbeth understood the toxicity of the thought life and its odd relationship with time. There was no antidote, no cure for his queen's dis-ease. She commits suicide. For good reason the play is known as a tragedy.

Years ago, I wrote a song with these lyrics:

Oh, to recall with tears those things forgotten,
Ghosts that remain, a hunger that survives,
A nameless ache that haunts the memory
For these things there is no language but a cry.

—"NO LANGUAGE BUT A CRY"

I can't remember what I was thinking when I wrote that, but I must have been brooding over these same issues, over my own rooted sorrows. More prayer than lyric, it summoned God. It invited him in. He offered me flight into timelessness, that share of him that gave me redemption from the past and all its claims on me, all its imaginary threats, all its deep and hidden poisons. He was…no, he *is* sufficient antidote.

I do not have to be a slave to time. I can enjoy a healthy detachment to the clock. I can also appreciate the beauty of things behind me, things I do not wish to forget, held firmly in the record of my memory.

We live in a world dominated by schedules, a responsible world overrun with demands and deadlines, an adult world of imperatives and lists we cannot ignore or rid ourselves of. Still, there is a place we may enter that is timeless, a place we may enter with all the permissions heaven can grant, where we may set aside all our obligations to time, where we may resume innocence again, a place near the Father where we can find contentment, where eternity is easy, where Eden is remembered in us, where hope and faith may rest their labors, where love may replenish itself, find its source and spring, a place where worship may flourish in its natural habitat. It is as close as the next act of kindness, the next soft kiss of love.

● ● ● ● ● ● ● ● ● a prayer of reminiscence ● ● ● ● ● ● ● ●

When we were kids, we hardly noticed it. We lived for our distractions and for something that came to us in the eager light of morning. We were the true mystics without the burden of explanation. And we knew nothing yet of clocks. They were just faces on the wall, benign, funny, round. They said nothing we could understand. But all that changed as we got older. Those same faces took on a more stern appearance—inflexible, oppressive. We stepped in formation to a new rhythm, the unnatural rhythm of ticking things—alarms, schedules, mechanical life. The droning day took something from us with each passing moment and put something colorless in our lives, consigning bold innocence to the memory of lost and unprofitable things. And we didn't see it coming. Redeem the hours, Lord. Overrule time. Cleanse my heart of its debris, my mind of all its contamination, all its corruption, all its "written troubles." Put to silence the illusions that charm me, that dull the life of devotion in me. Some are old and well practiced. Let me be a slave to time no longer. Let time be servant instead to me that I may discover the moments for what they are, how precious they are numbered. I want to make the best of those left to me. Reconcile "what is" with "what was," in the hope of what will be.

In Christ, who calls time to account, Christ, the antidote, my access to what is timeless. Amen.

May love begin to disclose the lies,
to unweave the fictions of your life and the many illusions
that have held them together, rendering them lifeless,
consigning them among voiceless and forgotten things.
May your soul be restored to the beauty of its origins.
May it be cleansed of its former life, leaving only a
vague remembrance that death ever lived there
or had any dominion at all.

stick your head out the window if you don't believe me

I have learned to be content whatever the circumstances.

PHILIPPIANS 4:11

*You're blessed when you're content with
just who you are—no more, no less.*

MATTHEW 5:5 MSG

True love is its own satisfaction.

BERNARD OF CLAIRVAUX
ON LOVING GOD

AM NOT SURE THERE IS A BETTER IMAGE of contentment than that of the dog with her head out the window of a car moving at any speed. Speed is never the issue with a dog unless she is chasing something or running toward someone. Contentment has no pace. And if my dogs were governed by anything that might resemble an emotion or state of mind, it was contentment.

Why do they stick their heads out the window? Truth is, neither the vet nor the behavioral scientist can tell you. You would be better off asking the dog.

The Oxford English Dictionary (OED) uses words such as "pleasure, delight, gratification" to describe contentment, along with "the action of satisfying; the process of being satisfied; satisfaction."[1] But if you get a good look at the dog's face, that definition doesn't come close. It is a bit, well, tame.

Here is a creature who knows only a few words, who is a total stranger to books, who has no respect for newspapers, making sport with one of the finest dictionaries in the English language. I love that.

I am not sure how such a prestigious dictionary as the OED would rewrite the definition. Some things defy expression. Maybe use more pictures. With a few modifications, it might read: *"I am dog! I am alive!"* Now *that's* contentment according to a dog. Life at capacity.

In truth I am sympathetic. Paul mentions "a man in Christ who… was caught up into the third heaven," to paradise, and such a man had no words to describe what he heard. Description stuck in his throat:

> He heard inexpressible things, things that man is not per-
> mitted to tell.
>
> —2 CORINTHIANS 12:4

A dog might have said, "Stick your head out the window and see for yourself." The paradise our dogs enjoyed was real to them. The happy look on their faces most of the time had no exclamation point, no excesses of any kind, no ceremony, just the calm enthusiasm and joy of a ride in the car, which was paradise enough. It was of no larger consequence than that. Such profound happiness at such little cost.

If you look into the eyes of a dog with her head out the window you'll see evidence of deep agreement between the dog and life. This agreement is what I want to explore, for in it is the source of true happiness.

the hidden text

There is an event that takes place deep within the confines of the human heart. Perhaps the word "event" is poorly chosen. I am not sure it is an *event*. I am not sure just what to call it, for the exchanges between God and man remain a mystery and defy our attempts to explain. Explanation is irrelevant anyway. Love, as we already know, is its own explanation, even as it is its own reward.

Anyway, such an "event" is so deep and so fixed, that on your best day (or your worst) you cannot unsettle it or chase it away. When Jesus says he will be with you always, he means what he says.[2]

The following is a simple illustration, and yet it helps me understand the life of God within me, that part of him within me that is *irrevocable*. If something is irrevocable, it is something…

> that cannot be recalled. That cannot be called, brought, fetched, or taken back; that is beyond recall or recovery. That cannot be revoked, repealed, annulled, or undone; unalterable, irreversible.
>
> **—OXFORD ENGLISH DICTIONARY**

By the way, the word "fetched" in the above is not my word. It is an OED word. Maybe they have it more together than I suspect.

Place a single drop of food coloring—something dark, like red or blue—into a glass of water. Give it a moment. Let the elements mingle, saturate. Now try to get that drop back. It can't be done. This simple illustration shows me the certainty by which God is joined to me, how he disperses himself in me, and by a unity that cannot be called back, one that I hardly understand.

As I have said, *love's whole idea is union, the lightness of true possession.* Once God has possession, once his life mingles with our own, there is no taking it back, there is no changing one's mind. We can give it our best try, but only to our misery, deep and thorough. The elements in our little illustration are simply obeying nature, doing what liquids do—or at least what *compatible* liquids do. They share elements. The mutuality is profound and in this case visible.

For you and me, to be joined with God is written in our very design. To live the devoted life, therefore, is to live in obedience to nature—our truer nature—to live in agreement with our Creator, to live in agreement with our blueprint, the original script. All the magnets within us draw us to the same conclusion, the same hidden text. Here too the mutuality is profound, and often visible.

The same is true with the calling of God. Once you have accepted it, once you have begun to submit to it, to feed upon it, to be seasoned by it, once your life has taken shape around it, there is no way to make it go away. I have tried. I have done everything in my power to resist it, to do other things, to say, "I am done with this now. I think I'll try something else." I was miserable in the process, though I cannot tell you why. My nights, sleepless; my days, droning and shapeless; all meaning obscured.

I know better now. The life of God is irrevocable. He would like nothing better than for all noticeable distinctions to disappear, that you and I be so united with him, so mingled, that there be such a confusion of elements, such a deep agreement, that it becomes difficult to tell just where we end and he begins.

* * * * * * * * * * * * * * * * * * * *

> *Dog and owner wind up thinking of each other*
> *as more or less part of themselves.*
>
> **ROGER GRENIER**
> ***THE DIFFICULTY OF BEING A DOG***

* * * * * * * * * * * * * * * * * * * *

This is the highest possible life, life as it was meant to be lived, life with your head stuck out the window, your eyes aglow, groovin', traveling at the speed of ordinary life. This is the kind of contentment King David knew, and John the Beloved, and the man of the tombs.[3] Even Savannah.

No, there is no getting it back. I am not sure I'd want *it* back, whatever *it* is. I am in love too deep to consider any other option. If you are not convinced that God is this intrusive, this invasive, that he does not meddle this deeply, that his resolve is not this intense and thorough, that his conquest is not that replete, that his finality is not quite that final, that his eyes do not have adequate range, read Psalm 139...maybe even twice. *Oh LORD, you have searched me and you know me."*

The word "know" here is עָדַי, *yada'* (yaw-dah'). It is the same word used in Genesis 4:1: "And Adam *knew* Eve his wife; and she conceived." I am not sure a relationship can get much closer than that, as mutual, or as creative.

can there be such a world?
The dogs had become our teachers long before we were aware that they

had become our teachers. It reminds me of a line from Jane Austen's *Pride and Prejudice*. Darcy is in love, and he is hardly aware of it before it is too late to do anything about it: "I was in the middle before I knew that I had begun." I think Jane was on to something.

When God is in pursuit, when he calls with all his tenderness, some remote part of us responds. Deep nature turns to its source. Deep memory is aroused. *Deep calls unto deep.* Our truest, most genuine humanity is raised from a type of slumber and wakens. God becomes the sun in our eyes. Often we find ourselves in the middle of it, hardly knowing it had even begun. Like poor Darcy, nothing is ever the same. Our whole being is, by conquest, changed forever.

To live in agreement with life comes easy for the dog. The dog is being what she was created to be—a dog. Nature cannot help but be what it is, and neither can the dog. There is an agreement between them, and by an order that was set in motion at creation. It is written in the code that makes a dog a dog.

A dog can squeeze the most out of life because of that. She lives in harmony with her own nature, living within the rule of dog, and she also enjoys harmony with the world around her because of these things. She doesn't trouble her psychology with options, as we are given to do. She is not motivated by anything other than being a dog. And this awareness is so interfused with everything else, she doesn't burden herself thinking about it. By being herself, by finding contentment in being herself, she can ask the same of nature around her, and nature is willing to comply.

Nature defaults to itself. Nature is most kind to her own, to those who understand her, to those who obey her rules. Nature becomes the dog's friend because they understand each other. The agreement is a mutual one. It is not difficult to see why the dog's contentment is so complete, so pure.

Happy comes easy to the dog, and she is satisfied with the least of provisions.

The same is true about the dog and her master. She lives in agreement with her master, and that agreement is the source of her deep contentment. This is possible because she lives within the boundaries her devotion demands of her. A mutual conformity exists between her and her master, a kind of contract she has voluntarily bound herself to simply because her master's happiness is her first thought.

> Deep memory is aroused. Deep calls unto deep. Our truest, most genuine humanity is raised from a type of slumber and wakens. God becomes the sun in our eyes. Often we find ourselves in the middle of it hardly knowing it had even begun.

The seasoned dog, the mature dog, knows these things. She thinks of little else actually. She loves her master more than she loves herself, more than he loves himself, and because of this, she is always conscious of keeping within the lines to please her master, which is her first priority. This is another reason the dog will show such severity of devotion even with an unkind master. She gives herself no options. Indeed, she cannot choose.

The dog's love for her master is more about who the master *is* than what he *does*. This is the natural order of love, the *logos* that clarifies it. It is not incorrect to say the dog's master is the architect of her happiness, the locus of her contentment. He sets the tone. He defines the limits. He determines all measures, proportion, and intensity of rewards—and punishments—when necessary. All dimensions are his alone. The dog knows this, and by her compliance, by her own instinctual need to submit, by her delight to make her master happy, the surrender no longer flows just one way but two. The surrender between the dog and master becomes mutual.

The master, within his own dominion, within his own margins of power, perhaps not even being aware of it, surrenders himself to the dog. And the dog knows it. Again, it is easy to understand her contentment. When the dog lives within these limits, or within the articles of agreement, it brings contentment that is as pleasurable—well, almost as pleasurable—for the master as it is for the dog.

I believe the same can be said of you and me. God seeks pleasure in man. Eden *(pleasure)* was named before Adam was put there. The anticipation existed in God's own heart. The mutuality, the sharing of joys, the deep unity, the lightness of true possession, the shared bliss, the singularity was all God's idea.

He made man in his own image. What was he thinking? Perhaps, "I like the idea of who I am, so let us create others like ourself, so the enjoyment can blossom, flourish. Can there be such a world, such a mimic of heaven?" On day six, the day he made man, he said, "Be fruitful and increase in number." God, from his own contentment, desired to replicate himself, to make his contentment even more content, to people the Earth with those of his own reflection. "Let us make man in our image, in our likeness."[4]

The artist creates by summoning up or calling forth from the content of his own soul. That sounds cliché, but I think you get my point. There is a type of unrest within the artist that demands a reckoning, a discontent that broods inside him that must be resolved. Our best books, paintings, songs, innovations of thought, inventions, are all drawn with the same ladle. Not unlike God at creation, the artist gives shape to what was formless, gives meaning to it, and emerges peacefully with an end product that reflects him more perfectly. A drawing or painting by Leonardo da Vinci is stamped with his peculiar image, that which is recognizable and separates him from all other artists. Before that there was just a blank canvas.

· · · · · · · · · · · · · · · · · · ·

One must have chaos in oneself to be able
to give birth to a dancing star.
FRIEDRICH NIETZSCHE
THUS SPAKE ZARATHUSTRA

· · · · · · · · · · · · · · · · · · ·

Hosea was told to marry a woman of sale, a prostitute, and he did just that.[5] There was meaning in the very act. Everything God touches, whatever he says or does, is replete with meaning. All creation has a voice.[6] The message, the prophecy Hosea was to declare, was scripted into his life. It was the living metaphor that made Hosea understand God in a way that was profound, complete, as thorough as thorough can possibly get. Things written in a man's blood, in the peculiar metachemistries of his heart, are not easily ignored. Eventually they must be accounted for. Ask Jonah.

In the beginning, creation was "formless and empty." Made by God, it did not yet reflect him. "And the Spirit of God moved upon the face of the waters."[7] As only he could, he saw the beauty in it, and yet there was work to do. To the formless and empty he gave light and order. To the void he gave rule and movement. Love operates by the same editorial principle. Here is another way to say it:

> In love there comes a moment when we begin to suspect the emerging of a truer form of ourselves, a liberation from all counterfeits and all imitations, when we realize that love sees with the eye of an artist, as one who toils for perfection and detail. For you were His first thought, His good idea put to the labor of creation, His deep intent come to life. You were the unrest in Him, for until His inmost desire brought forth the humanity nested within it, He did not rest. He toiled and took from the vast reserves of His soul all the beauty and divinity compressed within it and scattered it upon a new and unsuspecting universe. He busied Himself with preparation, even as a groom prepares His house for the day of visitation. You were His first and honored guest. Never despair of who you are. Love has a different idea of you altogether.
>
> In Christ, when love freed itself, when the unquiet in God was quiet again. Amen.
>
> —DAVID TEEMS, *TO LOVE IS CHRIST, JANUARY 23*

agreement

Agreement is one of the most powerful aspects of our psychology. Our lives are shaped by our agreements. Some are natural, some exist outside our nature and are the greatest impediments to the devoted life. Some exist outside the law of life. Some are harmful.

While many agreements we live by are among the most difficult things to change, God remains a God of possibility. He put in us the capacity to change. If not, he never would have used the word "repent," a word that, in spite of its weight, simply means to change one's mind, a correction, an afterthought.[8]

Take shame, for instance. For shame to have power over me, I must give my consent. I must agree to believe what it says about me, to live by its standards. Shame asks certain things of me, demands certain responses, certain judgments, evokes certain facial expressions. It alters and commands the way I perceive, and I am slave to its requests—that is, if I agree to be.

What is worse is that I may not be aware that I am submitted to such an ugly boss. It is a fairly classic consideration of human behavior, particularly with shame, or any agreement that has become old in us or well-rehearsed. If our submission is thorough enough, shame becomes a living thing, an active part of us, not unlike any other disease or insidious parasite.

In a culture that celebrates the thin, the rich, and the beautiful, that makes a fetish of youth and maligns old age, a culture where image is everything, it is not difficult to see there might be casualties. We have seen the evidence on *Dr. Phil* and *Oprah*. In this context, shame becomes a tool of commerce. It often drives the machine. The contract is one-sided and nonnegotiable.

. . . .

Those who look to him are radiant; their faces
are never covered with shame.
PSALM 34:5

. . . .

Shame behaves with animal subtlety. It makes no spectacle of itself. Retiring, fleeting, shrinking. Something settles on our faces, on our countenance, in the light about us, in our posture, though we are often unaware of its authority over us. People around us seem to pick up on it, often before we do. Not unlike love, many of the agreements we make are underway before we are really aware of them.

Shame puts the droop in a smile, sadness and deflation that shows not only in our eyes, but in our choice of words, in the music our voice makes, things we cannot counterfeit. We may act in any fashion we choose, but shame has a way of expressing itself, of proving its dominance. It takes little discernment for others to sense it about us. An uncomfortable presence, it often arouses flight instead of further engagement. It also has the power to trigger similar agreements in others.

At the positive extreme, our agreement with God operates much the same way, only with better consequence. It is a garment we wear, translucent, bright and yet not blinding, conspicuous and yet not loud. It is the lift in a smile. It is a light about us, though we may be the last to know.

• •

They will sparkle in his land like jewels in a crown.
How attractive and beautiful they will be!
ZECHARIAH 9:16-17

• •

the devoted life is a
stick-your-head-out-the-window
kind of life

Contentment is the default condition of the devoted life. Is it an easy life? No, it is not. Is it a safe life? Far from it. If the life of Christ or the lives of his followers have taught us anything, it is that the devoted life is a life of risk. The way is narrow and steep. The surrender is absolute. But it is also as beautiful as it is costly. The contentment is deep and thorough. And fear has no place in it. Again, sometimes you just have to stick your head out the window and see for yourself.

Contentment, like all other aspects of God, is alive and active. It serves as a husbandman who tends the good soil and all sleeping seed. It acts as teacher and guide, as watchman and groom. Contentment inhabits our words, our actions, our inwardness, our private thoughts, all transactions with life without and within. It acts as sentinel over our dreams, a rearguard and prop to all we attempt. It settles over us with all the agreement of heaven, all the beatitude of Christ. Can there be such a world, such a mimic of heaven?

It is that simple, and we hardly need the dog to show us that. But there is something else.

The devoted life is a life of contentment, yes, but the reward does not end there. To live in agreement with God is to live within the rule of love. It means that my soul operates according to the rule of him who gave order to the unordered universe, who fashioned me accordingly, by and for his pleasure.

* * * * * * * * * * * * * * * * * *

Love is the eternal law whereby the universe was created and is ruled.

BERNARD OF CLAIRVAUX
ON LOVING GOD

* * * * * * * * * * * * * * * * * *

I show compassion because God is compassionate. Where he loves, I love. This is agreement. Where he shows kindness, I show kindness. It is a "thy people shall be my people"[9] kind of living mutuality. This affects all particulars of life, public and private. This living agreement touches the minutiae of life with as much verve as it does the grander schemes.

In time, even the word "agreement" becomes unnecessary or redundant. It is absorbed into life. Whether it be the emotional life, money, politics, the Christian man or woman lives in a balance of design, an evenness according to the rule and measure of God. God is the locus, the strong immovable center in which our lives are joined.

once I get it, what do I do with it?

Agreement comes by way of an exchange of information, a living awareness that is never static but always in play, the continuous current between God and man, or, for the sake of our metaphor, between master and dog. The cue the dog watches for, the permission she seeks for her contentment is all in the power of her god, her master. She studies those cues. She makes them her life.

But what about the rest of us? In these uneasy times, where is contentment to be found? And how am I to hold on to it once it is mine?

I will not attempt to suggest what will work for everyone, but there are certain dynamics of agreement that are fairly stable. My wife loves a good list. It doesn't matter what it is, it just gives her a sense of comfort to look at one. It has the appearance of order, of conscientious thought and deliberation. I, on the other hand, have always had an aversion to lists. They are rather boring and charged with obligation. Even so, God made a few lists of his own—the Ten Commandments, for one, and the ten plagues of Egypt. So I am willing to try something new, but I'll make mine brief.

The action you take is all your own. Use whatever invention you might, whatever your heart teaches you. Agreement with God is the ultimate goal, and these are the essentials.

1. Know what makes your master happy, and adjust your life accordingly.

2. Do whatever it takes to accomplish #1.

I said it was brief. But too simple or incomplete? Not really. My contentment is in my master. If I love my master, my desire is to make him happy, and in that, I am happy. And my happiness is not a superficial one, but one of unimaginable depth and reach.

If for some reason my list doesn't work for you, or you get flustered, you might try turning around three times and lying down—regrouping, refining, regathering. If all else fails, stick your head out the window of your car and let the wind blow in your face. It might put everything into perspective.

• • • • • • • • a prayer of contentment • • • • • • • •

I am a stranger to all other happiness but you, Lord. I have deceived myself long enough. The things that brought me happiness, like the happiness itself, were an illusion. I renounce my former vision of life, all unwholesome agreements, those I am aware of and those I am not. I do not do this lightly, for I have been under foreign government most of my life, and to cast off rule and old, useless habit are difficult for me. Make your conquest absolute, Lord, for this is not a thing I can do alone. I have neither the strength nor the resolve. I have sought happiness everywhere but at its source. You have provided the rule of love, and within its margins you have set me free, and in this freedom I am happy. Help me understand this blessedness, this joy, this uncommon felicity—to cherish it, to set a guard over it, to be jealous over it. To understand how powerful it is, how deathless, and yet how fragile, how light, how easy. For all your severity, for all the thunder at your command, all your great power and charge, you watch over the little things, the insignificant things no one notices. You are the God of comfort, who made the butterfly and the wren, who first thought of clouds and put whispers in the wind. I am yours in lightness and severity. May blessedness be my teacher. May love alone be my rule.

In Christ, the rule of love. Amen.

May your life be stick-your-head-out-the-car-window-
let-the-wind-blow-in-your-face kind of good!

the joy of being who i am

I have come that they may have life,
and have it to the full.
JOHN 10:10

They are perfectly content to be who they are, without torturing
themselves with alternatives: They love being dogs.
JEFFREY MASSON
DOGS NEVER LIE ABOUT LOVE

Not to accept and love and do God's will
is to refuse the fullness of my existence.
THOMAS MERTON
NEW SEEDS OF CONTEMPLATION

A DOG HAS A CLEARER UNDERSTANDING of what it means to be a dog than you and I have an understanding of what it means to be human. Not only that, she is happy about it. It is difficult to imagine a dog musing about being a dog or writing about the "virtues of being me." She might see this as a waste of her time. I suspect she gives it little thought, if any. Self is very plain to her. Not only is it plain to her, but she lives with a healthy detachment from it. She is free to invest her energies in more worthwhile pursuits. It is a big life, after all, and there is little time to get it all in.

To say that the dog lives at capacity is to say she lives in that enviable state of absolute selfhood. Awareness and acceptance live in agreement together. She knows who she is, and she accepts who she is without debate. She can do this because she is fully aware of what that means, of what selfhood is. Life takes on a glow of authenticity. You can see it in her bounce, in the buoyancy she brings to life.

Her perceptions are not distorted by vanity or other psychological saboteurs. Shame has no voice inside her. She can approach life with concord and with hopeful anticipation because of the clarity that such awareness affords her. If speech were an option, you might hear her say, *"I am happy to be me because I know what that means. I am at peace with myself. I know where I fit in the scheme of things. I acknowledge nothing that frustrates me from being me. And I can love you fully because I live fully. My surrender is absolute because I understand myself absolutely."*

> Self behaves rather like a god, and because of this our allegiance becomes obscured and divided. One master per dog—that is the rule.

Of course, her god is a visible one.

For you and me, life is a bit more complex. We have psychological knots and tangles the dog will, with all probability, never suffer. If love seems elusive, if it seems aloof or a bit too much work, it is usually in proportion to our attachment to or our absorption in self. Self behaves rather like a god, and because of this our allegiance can become obscured and divided. One master per dog—that is the rule.

The God we serve is an invisible God. How different life might be otherwise. How much simpler it might be to understand who we are before him if the veil were removed, if we could see him, get close enough to touch him, if all restraints were loosed, all restrictions lifted, if we could speak directly to him and get an immediate response. But we are not given that advantage.

We are given one way to know God. I did not make the rules, but I am afraid it is just that simple. Not only that, but if my true identity is hidden in God, and it is, and if there is only one way to know God, then there is but one way for me to know myself, and that is love. There is no other path:

> Whoever does not love does not know God,
> because God is love.
>
> —1 JOHN 4:8

In *New Seeds of Contemplation*, Thomas Merton suggests that holiness is being ultimately who we are, that authenticity and sanctification are one and the same thing, that salvation itself is conjunctive with finding one's truest self. The secret of our identity is hidden in God. God bears "in Himself the secret of who I am."

> The secret of my identity is hidden in the love and mercy of God. But whatever is in God is really identical with Him, for His infinite simplicity admits no division and no distinction. Therefore I cannot hope to find myself anywhere except in Him.[1]

In what continues to unfold like a lyric, Merton writes,

> God utters me like a word containing a partial thought of Himself. A word will never be able to comprehend the voice that utters it. But if I am true to the concept that God utters in me, if I am true to the thought of Him I was meant to embody, I shall be full of His actuality and find Him in myself, and find myself nowhere. I shall be lost in Him: that is, I shall find myself. I shall be "saved."[2]

a fascination for mirrors

In spite of the occasional foam rubber reindeer antlers or some other indignity, maybe a silly birthday hat, mouse ears, or some article of clothing from one of the boys, self-image was never a problem for Oreo. She got the joke and laughed with us. She was happy to be caught up in the spirit of the moment. She knew there was kindness in it. She trusted her god. She knew the play was warm, that community was engaged, that it was filled with regard and mutual respect. Plus she enjoyed the sound of our laughter.

As beautiful as she was, vanity never seemed to be a problem for her. She never developed a fascination for mirrors. None of our dogs did.

Salem, the only male of the three, betrayed a certain animal pride whenever attention was drawn his way, especially if Benita was involved. His bowl, his bandana, his rawhide bone were all part of the spectacle.

He would turn occasionally while eating to make sure Benita was watching. Or me. *"Aren't you proud? I'm all yours."* Forgive this anthropomorphism, but it just looked that way to us. And there was Savannah, who seemed to remain in a perpetual state of swoon whenever I was around. She had no other attachments. No favorite food, no favorite toy, nothing—only me. Their personalities were distinct. Life was anything but dull.

This notion of selfhood is a slippery one. Where the dog might be able to ignore it or at least put it aside as a trifle, you and I do not. We are somewhat fascinated by it. Nonetheless, it should be handled with a measure of caution—in spite of the entitlement of the times. It is not unlike a balancing act, a thing to be approached with respect, and yet lightly. Toxicity lies at the extremes. We have all seen the evidence.

Scripture commands that we deny ourselves,[3] that we surrender the *self* as unto death. It says that in order to find myself, I must first lose myself.[4] But what if I am not sure who or what I am supposed to lose or find or deny? Life is enough of a scramble for identity.

Not only that, but we are commanded to love our neighbors as we love ourselves, suggesting that we are indeed to love ourselves. We are to love that thing we have just lost and denied and found again. Would somebody please help? In the confusion and in this grappling for identity, it becomes easy to put on a counterfeit, to create the narrative myself, to live by an idea of myself because the reality is way too much work and way too difficult to understand.

to be or not to be

According to many literary scholars and critics, the greatest achievement in the English language to date is Shakespeare's *Hamlet*, both the character and the play. But whatever opinion we might have, if any, there has hardly been a literary character more alive, more intelligent, more human, more palpable, more perfectly flawed, more tragic than Prince Hamlet. Other than the King James Bible, the English language has yet to offer the world anything quite like him or the play that features him.

There is something quite different about *Hamlet* that separates

the play and the prince from all literature, that had no literary ante-
cedent, that was quite original—his *inwardness*, his possession of *self*,
and his ability to give it speech. Hamlet brought inner monologue to
the modern stage, that literary device of overhearing oneself, of giving voice to thought.

This makes Hamlet useful because he also asks the question of
questions, perhaps the most human of questions, and most everyone,
whether a devotee of Shakespeare or not, is familiar with the question Hamlet asks himself: "To be, or not to be…" And I think he is
right. That *is* the question, is it not? It may be the ultimate question,
the quintessential question of life. Forget any suggestion of suicide
in the play for the moment, any existential or ontological argument,
and simply consider the notion of *what does it mean to be me?* That is
question enough.

*When I look in the mirror, can I explain what I see? Do I really know
the person staring back at me? Does he or she live deliberately, with purpose and intent, or cautiously to avoid harm or detection? Do I take my
steps in this world with hesitation or with command? With uncertainty or
with belief? Do I live in the shallows of life or in the deeps? Is my identity
bound in my job, in things I am known to do? Or in my holdings, my
wealth? Am I a mere creation, an invention? Do I even know? Have I
ever considered such a thing before now? This person in the mirror before
me moves when I move. It speaks with my voice. It walks with my gait.
It must be me. Or is it?*

One of the characters in *Hamlet* is a meddling old man named
Polonius, who gives some last-minute counsel to his son, Laertes, who
is leaving Denmark to return to school. Among a litany of other things,
Polonius says,

> This above all: to thine own self be true,
> And it must follow, as the night the day,
> Thou canst not then be false to any man.
>
> —WILLIAM SHAKESPEARE,
> *HAMLET, I, III,78-80*

It's like the Golden Rule—only not.[5] The Golden Rule convoluted
perhaps or maybe amplified. It has the weight of a proverb, and while

it is not found in Scripture, it is still a trustworthy piece of advice. If I am true to myself, it follows that I can be true to others, for I am true indeed. But don't be fooled. It is not as easy as it sounds. To be true "to thine own self" implies that one knows what that means, that one is sufficiently aware or has adequate possession of *self*.

I cannot be true to something I am unfamiliar with or that I know falsely because, in spite of my sincerity, my approach will be just as false. If I create an image of myself over the years, if I live by some counterfeit, even unknowingly or with the best intentions, then to be true to such a counterfeit is to remain true to something that is simply not true. And something that is not true is something that is not real. It is imagined. Therefore, the God I seek will be just as false because all things are false to me. My devotion is as much an illusion as he is.

This is more common than you might think. Many of us have created God after our own image, a God that talks like us, that judges like us, that looks like us, that shares our political views, that suits all our particulars, and so on.

authorship

A rather disturbing truth is that many of us live according to some personal mythology. Knowingly or unknowingly we create the notion of who we are, or perhaps it is created for us. It may be a pleasant or an unpleasant fiction, but either way it is a fiction, a fable, better left to novelists and playwrights. Each fiction demands a kind of faith to sustain it. Indeed, we develop a rule of belief, a theology of sorts. It is our agreement, our consent, that makes the difference. Many of these scripts are old in us and resist change. This is an unfortunate condition of life.

I suspect here too the dog fares better. She might chase an occasional shadow around the room and maybe even her own tail now and then, but as a rule she is not led by her illusions as you and I are given to do. In *Dogs Never Lie About Love*, Jeffrey Masson makes this observation:

> It is possible that we begrudge the dog his freedom to be
> exactly what he was meant to be: a dog. So often I will see

Sasha or Rani or Sima roll over and over in thick green grass, with a look of sheer delight on their faces, and I will think they are doing exactly what a dog was meant to do. How much harder to say of ourselves that we are doing what a human was meant to do, especially as nobody knows what that is.

It is not one we typically think of perhaps, but the greatest reward of the devoted life is the discovery, at last, of who we are. But this only *sounds* simple. The reality is quite different. Authentic selfhood demands a pioneering spirit—that willingness to meddle with the sleeping or the unexplored within us. The illusions that keep us hostage are strong ones. Many of us never break free of them. They are too comforting and too familiar. Our psychology feeds upon them, and we are hardly aware of it. The belief we have invested is too stubborn.

We are not very good at recognizing illusions, least of all the ones we cherish about ourselves.

THOMAS MERTON
NEW SEEDS OF CONTEMPLATION

Wouldn't it be nice to live in the certainty of your own identity, to know with confidence who you are, with no makeup, no gloss or makeover, no image enhancement—just you, plain you, the lowest common denominator you, you to the essence, you at capacity, you without the propaganda and spin, just this bright reflected image of the divine—clear, transparent, alive, available, approachable, with all the amenities of sonship? That is a long question indeed.

This is not to suggest a preoccupation with *me*, but selfhood—healthy, inspired selfhood, life-enhancing selfhood—is a gift from God, a God of love. You could say it proceeds from him. He thought it up in the first place.

To define "authentic," the Oxford English Dictionary uses words such as "original, first-hand, prototypical (as opposed to copied)—real, actual, genuine (as opposed to imaginary, pretended)." It doesn't get much clearer than that. If you are familiar with the OED, you know it is quite an exhaustive dictionary, probably the finest in the English language. Read on:

> proceeding from its reputed source or author; of undisputed origin, genuine. (Opposed to counterfeit, forged, apocryphal.)

To live an authentic life, therefore, is to live as the original author of that life has designed it. Any other life is *counterfeit* (a fraudulent imitation), *forged* (a deceptive copy, particularly with regard to signature), or *apocryphal* (spurious, doubtful).

Scripture refers to Jesus as the *"author* and perfecter of our faith"[6] (the *"author and finisher* of our faith," if the sonority of the King James Version is more to your taste). In Acts 3:15, Peter refers to Jesus Christ as the *"author* of life." Hebrews refers to Jesus as "the *author* of their salvation."[7]

I love the craft of writing. I have studied it for years and will continue to study it. I have read extensively about the craft and continue to feed on the major craftsmen simply because I love books. I am ever a student of the written word. Most writers I know are afflicted with the same ailment. In most cases it is incurable.

> Authentic selfhood demands a pioneering spirit— that willingness to meddle with the sleeping or the unexplored within us.

Enthusiasm is part of the psychology of authorship. I'm not sure any book or any worthy piece of art is accomplished without it. Actually, I am not sure there is a more enthusiastic bunch in the world than artists and writers, which includes the whole odd cast—poets, songwriters, screenwriters, playwrights, novelists, and others who live by means of the word.

If I am enthusiastic about the craft and other authors are enthusiastic about it, I imagine the Author of authors is enthusiastic, if not even more so. Every author wishes for his book to have life, but *his* actually live and breathe. As great works of art do, each one reflects the author in its own specific way.

· ·

"Enthusiasm" has a Latin parentage, enthusiasmus,
which means "being possessed by a god."
OXFORD ENGLISH DICTIONARY

· ·

Any authorship of merit is usually achieved by a mix of pleasure and an intense labor to produce—a mix of delight, hard work, a deep knowledge of the craft, and a touch of something unknown even to the best of authors. The finished product is worth whatever suffering or hardship it demands. It is something you must wrestle out of you— an offspring, a prize, a thing of wonder.

With each book, each painting, each sculpture, each musical composition some piece of the author goes with it, some small share of himself, purchased with equal measures of agony and joy. It is indeed a labor of love. All his energy is summoned up, all his best. It is not something that can be rushed, but when it is done, his signature comes to rest on the work itself. Often if you know the work of a specific author, it is not difficult to discern his or her work from that of others.

I find it comforting to think of God as an author, a finisher, a perfecter. It comforts me even more to know he literally puts himself into his work, and that he does it so thoroughly. The signature he leaves is a living signature, the autograph of God, peculiar to him alone. It cannot be forged or imitated.

The finest painting of a sunset will never be more than a painting of a sunset. It will never change. It will have many admirers, but it will never live. The best it can do is mimic divine authorship. Da Vinci's *Mona Lisa* is a wonder, yes, but it is still a two-dimensional wonder, a wonder of old paint and genius.

The sunset I watched yesterday was much more than that. It was a living thing. It was fluid. It was lyrical. There was poetry and understatement in its movement. A single beam of dying light, a downy bloat of clouds, a sky that seemed to bleed. Moment to moment, from glory to glory, never dull, a playing out of some script and right before my eyes. Asking things of my senses that a painting cannot ask. Moving me in ways unknown to art.

Now *that* is authorship. And though I am more important to him than any spectacle of nature, he leaves nothing out. His signature is all around us. It is fluid. It is lyrical. The detail is immaculate as he is immaculate.

* * * * * * * * * * * * * * * * * * * *

I praise you because I am fearfully and wonderfully made.

PSALM 139:14

* * * * * * * * * * * * * * * * * * * *

His authorship is achieved as well by a mix of pleasure, intense labor, mystery, divinity, a deep knowledge of the craft, and a deep knowledge of the medium with which he works.

Each living volume—each life he authors—is a complete world unto its own, a vast teeming world discovered and undiscovered all at once, a unity unto itself, an original—each one an offspring, a prize, a thing of wonder, having no equal, no mimic. All his energy, all his creative stores, all of his best is summoned up and given flesh. His seal, his signature, rests upon each of them.

god is in the details

In making a book, or actually with any piece of writing, the first draft, for me at least, though it may have a fine moment or two, is for my eyes only. This is the draft I write with the door closed. This is the time when I step up to the plate and swing the hardest, all guts and glory. I might forget commas in a rush and make other foibles of syntax. I may fall flat over my own tripping participles. But in spite of any haste, and in spite of its rawness, it has within it all the original fire, that first pulse that gave it life. It also has the optimism, that bright, lovely insanity that made it glow white hot in my imagination.

I have at times, for the sake of pristine text or by distraction, actually lost the thing, doused it altogether. I have worked over something for so long that I chased all the first inspiration right out of it, playing Jezebel to my own Elijah. The result was a very clean piece of writing, but with no warmth, no life, nothing of the original fire.

If I am fortunate, I catch myself and recapture the slippery thing in a rewrite. It is a small madness many writers understand because we are dealing with uncertainty and raw inspiration at the same time. And that is why I bother. When it is right, there is nothing sweeter.

> The finest painting of a sunset will never be more than a painting of a sunset. It will never change. It will have many admirers, but it will never live. The best it can do is mimic divine authorship.

The door slowly opens.

You may have heard it said that the first impulse, the first word or thought, is usually the best one. Though not always, this is often true. The point is, as long as the piece retains its original inspiration, as long as it glows with its first heat, it has a chance to become all it was intended to become. It can be its purest self from the first intimation to the finished product.

The same is true for you. That original inspiration, that first fire, allows you to be your truest self. The finished product is nothing less than what was intended according to that first intimation, the original, nothing less than the inimitable, irrevocable, and unmistakable you. If you have somehow lost it, you can get it back. If you have squandered it or weren't sure what it was to begin with, it is within your reach. If you just can't see it, Jesus still heals the blind.

> We all, with unveiled face, beholding as in a mirror the glory of the Lord, are being transformed into the same image from glory to glory, just as by the Spirit of the Lord.
> —2 CORINTHIANS 3:18 NKJV

To live *without* the Author's signature is to live incompletely, unfinished. To live in ellipsis, in suspension, a life of "if onlys" or "what ifs." Both present and future become obscured, opaque. It is life out of center.

To live *with* his signature is to live life at capacity, a life of pure possibility, in the steady company of the attainable God. This is your truest, most genuine self. This is the holiness he demands of us.

Once my first draft is complete, I let it sit for a while, alone, in a kind of wilderness (usually a desk drawer). After enough time goes by, and after a bit of rewriting and rethinking, the last stage is the polish. This is the stage I love the best. Any author of worth will polish his manuscript again and again until it shines, until a harmony stretches from cover to cover, until all the lumps are gone, all imperfections are addressed and purged. It is a predatory impulse. A bit of ruthlessness helps. Only the author knows when it is ready. Something in his gut lets him know. There is a discernable hum that peels from the better lines, each one saturated with meaning and clarity.

This is the moment of finesse and virtuosity, and, yes, God *is* in the details.[8] He is always in the details. He never seems to take a vacation from the details. If you understand this, you will understand my gratitude. When the text is pliable, when it surrenders in his hands, when it softens under his touch, it becomes a thing of beauty: fluid, lyrical, and more alive and more animated than the sky at sunset. This is the stage when it turns into a book, a living thing, an original, a work the author is willing to present the world.

"a time to break down; a time to build up"

The most recognizable lyric of love in the English language, the one set of verses in Scripture we usually think of when we think of love— 1 Corinthians 13—is also a small treatise on perfection. This fascinates me. That love is integrally associated with design itself, with the architecture of life. We might even say love puts movement in the sculptor's wheel and the warm idea of you in his hands.

> Love is the logos, the central heat of inspiration, the primal cause, the unreason God reasons with.

Augustine spoke of God as a poet, and rightfully so.[9] Poet that he is, love put words in his mouth when he spoke creation into being. Love is the *logos*, the central heat of inspiration, the primal cause, the unreason God reasons with. It is a reduction, a trimming, a pruning, an articulating, a shaping, a voicing, a stripping away. Is God in the details? Is he any-where else?

> Love never fails. But where there are prophecies, they will cease; where there are tongues, they will be stilled; where there is knowledge, it will pass away. For we know in part and we prophesy in part, but when perfection comes, the imperfect disappears. When I was a child, I talked like a child, I thought like a child, I reasoned like a child. When I became a man, I put childish ways behind me. Now we see but a poor reflection as in a mirror; then we shall see face to face. Now I know in part; then I shall know fully, even as I am fully known.
>
> —1 CORINTHIANS 13:8-12

Love is my purification, my cleansing, my sanctification. Love is my maturation, my seasoning, my spiritual adulthood, my initiation, my ascent to a higher, truer life. Love is the agent, the broker of my truer freedom. Love is my liberation, my flight from the corruptions of this world. My immunity. My deep medicine. Love is the clarity I seek in the mirror.

This association of love and authorial design is replete throughout Scripture. Scripture is steeped in this twin theme. You hardly find one without the other.

Words like "righteous" or "righteousness" in any of its forms used to scare me. I thought them lumpy and unfair. I could not help but bristle at the words, tiptoe around them, and avoid using them if at all possible. There was an air of antiquity about them, of old author-ity that annoyed me. Pretension and puff. Even so, Scripture does not avoid them. Indeed, to make the point it labors to make, Scripture employs that word and words like it again and again. To cleanse me from "all unrighteousness," as it says, is simply to cleanse me of all that is *not* me.[10]

The word "righteous," until the sixteenth century, was literally "right-wise."[11] We might think "right way" or "right manner." According to my own editorial rule, there is *right* and there is *not right*. I try to purge my text of the latter, of all that is *not right*. Sometimes I succeed.

Love employs the same tactic, and with far more precision than I am capable. There is *right* and there is *not right*. One is compatible with love; one is not. And love never fails. God is the only author who gets it right every time.

No greater explanation is necessary. Love, then, is my ultimate reality, *the perfect me, the articulate me.* Once that is accomplished, once I am washed clean of all the excess and unnecessary, I am in paradise again—not outside the traffic of others, but indeed, in the teeming midst of them, in the thickets. I do not fear losing myself to the herd or the seductions of a culture that has nothing in common with my origins.

In the ugliest of worlds, in the most perilous or weariest of times, I am clothed in paradise. I am clothed in truth. I am clothed with myself. I can approach life in all its genuineness because I know what that means. Until that time, love labors in me. Detail by detail. Glory to glory. How does love do it? Simple. By being itself:

> I am the true vine, and my Father is the gardener. He cuts off every branch in me that bears no fruit, while every branch that does bear fruit he prunes so that it will be even more fruitful. You are already clean because of the word I have spoken to you. Remain in me, and I will remain in you. No branch can bear fruit by itself; it must remain in the vine. Neither can you bear fruit unless you remain in me.
>
> I am the vine; you are the branches. If a man remains in me and I in him, he will bear much fruit; apart from me you can do nothing. If anyone does not remain in me, he is like a branch that is thrown away and withers; such branches are picked up, thrown into the fire and burned. If you remain in me and my words remain in you, ask whatever you wish, and it will be given you. This is to my Father's glory, that you bear much fruit, showing yourselves to be my disciples.
>
> As the Father has loved me, so have I loved you. Now remain in my love. If you obey my commands, you will remain in my love, just as I have obeyed my Father's commands and remain in his love.
>
> —JOHN 15:1-10

Here again, love plays the architect, the builder. For God recognizes only himself. He made man in his likeness. As I am stripped of all that is *not right* or *not me*, his image becomes clearer. The lyric continues. My joy rises and expands and fills me to excess. This joy is my power, my strength.[12]

. . . .

I have told you this so that my joy may be in you and that your joy may be complete. My command is this: Love each other as I have loved you. Greater love has no one than this, that he lay down his life for his friends. You are my friends if you do what I command. I no longer call you servants, because a servant does not know his master's business. Instead, I have called you friends, for everything that I learned from my Father I have made known to you. You did not choose me, but I chose you and appointed you to go and bear fruit— fruit that will last. Then the Father will give you whatever you ask in my name. This is my command: Love each other.

JOHN 15:11-17

. . . .

Jesus speaks both of pruning and loving. The two seem inseparable. He speaks of tearing down and of building up, of stripping and of friendship, of joy and of giving your life for a friend. Love is the unreason that makes sense of it all. By the way, the same guy who said "God is in the details" also said "Less is more." His occupation? Architect.

out of my obscurity

Because creative genius is a mystery to most of us, maybe we think that by some trick of inevitability or by the whim of artistic evolution a *Hamlet* simply appears, a *Mona Lisa*, or a *Divine Comedy*. This is just not true. Often there is a price—and a heavy one.

Friendless and alone, Dante Alighieri (1265–1321) was exiled from his beloved Florence, separated from his wife and children forever. And it was in this condition as an outcast, as one cruelly stripped of his former life, that he wrote his *Commedia—The Divine Comedy*. Without this change in fortune there would have been no such work, no such Dante as we know him.

Something was shaken loose; something powerful stripped to its essence.

Not only that, Dante was moved by one great force in his life, that drove all his work, impelled as he was "by the love that moves the sun and the other stars."[13]

* *

Dante's patron, to whom he dedicated Paradiso, *was* Cangrande della Scala. *Cangrande means "big dog."*

* *

I have mentioned *Hamlet*, Shakespeare's great achievement. There is a story here as well. The poet's son, Hamnet, died three or so years before the play was written. The poet's father, John Shakespeare, died the year *Hamlet* was completed (1601). Mathematician I am not, but curious, yes. I think it at least fair to suggest that one of the greatest works of genius in the English language was written in a time of massive inward turbulence, a time of sorrow by a double measure of grief, grief for a beloved son only 11 years old and for a father the playwright adored all his life.

Love and grief conspired together to create his masterpiece, a play that examines the quintessential question of life, that asks questions of being, and of the basic meaning of personhood, rhapsodized by a prince whose intelligence seemed as lucid as it was wild.

Hamlet grieves throughout the play. In a way, he grieves for Shakespeare himself. It may be the prince who wears the customary black, but it is the poet who grieves. But instead of his senses being dulled, they are heightened, liberated, reduced to their purest expression. Hamlet's speech is distilled to a fine essence, to clarity. His awareness of self is acute, bitter, sharp—as I believe they were for Shakespeare himself.

* *

But I have that within me which passeth show;
These but the trappings and the suits of woe.
HAMLET

* *

Scholars may disagree with me perhaps. It is of little consequence. *Hamlet* is a fiction. But against all the sorrow of the make-believe prince there was a bright, deathless clarity about *Hamlet* unlike anything else Shakespeare wrote:

> Since my dear soul was mistress of her choice
> And could of men distinguish, her election
> Hath seal'd thee for herself; for thou hast been
> As one, in suffering all, that suffers nothing,
> A man that fortune's buffets and rewards
> Hast ta'en with equal thanks: and blest are those
> Whose blood and judgment are so well commingled,
> That they are not a pipe for fortune's finger
> To sound what stop she please. Give me that man
> That is not passion's slave, and I will wear him
> In my heart's core, ay, in my heart of heart,
> As I do thee.

—WILLIAM SHAKESPEARE,
HAMLET

My dogs loved *Hamlet*. Or they made me believe they did. They let me read as much as I wanted to them and quote my favorite passages. They never complained like my sons always did. They were a fine audience. Of course they slept through much of it. My wife says they just liked the sound of my voice. But they loved Shakespeare. I am convinced of that. After all, if you take a closer look at Scripture, it is not so kind to dogs. Just over 40 references and not one good one. Dogs fare much better in Shakespeare. They are much safer there. Salem particularly liked that "dog shall have his day" thing Hamlet says. Truth is, I think they only appeared to like Shakespeare to make me happy.

Maybe violent love was the code that unlocked something in Shakespeare, that clarified something otherwise vague or opaque, something secluded, hidden in his depths. Perhaps what we call genius is merely the bright clarity of our origins liberated, unbound, let out of its box. Perhaps what we call genius is not genius at all, but merely the expression of something profoundly human, primal, authentic, unspoiled.[14] Maybe there is a Hamlet in each of us. Hopefully without the mess.

Only love can clear away the years of false life, all the onion-peel accumulations, all the substances that have kept so much within us mute, unvoiced. The following is an excerpt from Lebanese poet and artist Kahlil Gibran. In this lyric and in a language worthy of it, he illuminates love's attention to detail:

> For even as love crowns you so shall he crucify you.
> Even as he is for your growth so is he for your pruning.
> Even as he ascends your height and caresses your tenderest
>   branches that quiver in the sun,
> So shall he descend to your roots and shake them in their
>   clinging to the earth.
> Like sheaves of corn he gathers you unto himself.
> He threshes you to make you naked.
> He sifts you to free you from your husks.
> He grinds you to whiteness.
> He kneads you until you are pliant;
> And then he assigns you to his sacred fire, that you may
>   become sacred bread for God's sacred feast.
> All these things shall love do unto you that you may know
>   the secrets of your heart, and in that knowledge become
>   a fragment of Life's heart.
> But if in your fear you would seek only love's peace and
>   love's pleasure,
> Then it is better for you to cover your nakedness and pass
>   out of love's threshing floor,
> Into the seasonless world where you shall laugh, but not all
>   your laughter, and weep, but not all your tears.
>
> —KAHLIL GIBRAN, *"ON LOVE," THE PROPHET*

Even as God does, love reduces or distills to essences. It has the power to reduce me to my lowest common denominator, to the truest version of who I am. In this reduction, this negation of the imaginary self, my life truly begins. Washed clean of all counterfeit and pretension, I am lifted out of my own obscurity. In love, I welcome the stranger home who is a stranger no more.

I can love my neighbor as myself because love has dominion in me at last, and the more I love, the more present God becomes. The more present God becomes, the greater my joy. I can love my neighbor purely because I know myself purely. My neighbor and I are drawn together in the great magnetism of God's love. We enter by way of community into the pleasure of the Lord, the Eden prepared for us.

Life at capacity can be defined, therefore, as *self fully realized*, that enviable state that allows the full expression of my humanity and God's divinity within me, the two reconciled, abiding and laboring agreeably together, continually, outside my awareness, the cooperation of two realms joined in me. It is the author, after all, polishing, polishing, and polishing some more. I can give all because I know what "all" is. I can plunge happily and headlong into the mystery before me, living continually in the pleasure of him who thought me up in the first place.

● ● ● ● ● ● ● ● ● **a prayer of wakefulness** ● ● ● ● ● ● ● ●

You are the sun in my eyes, Lord, the day that breaks on all my sleeping senses. Search me until you see yourself. I am hopeful clay. And in the yielding, in the undoing, in the unraveling of all my fictions, in the unspinning of all my webs, in the letting go, I will know with certainty just who I am. Let joy overcome me, even as sight given to a man born blind. Let gladness and thanksgiving be my twin witnesses in a cynical world. Let redemption, like worship, be a continuous event in my life. Author me into gladness. Put yourself into this peculiar work. For I am no less a gospel, a love letter written by the sure hand of majesty. I am a poem forming in the mouth of my God, a psalm ascending, an ecstasy rising in the midst of all my disenchantments. I am contentment in the heart of deity. I am myself. I am awake.

In Christ, my wakefulness. Amen.

●●.●.●

May you never fear moments of tenderness,
in giving or in receiving, nor the authority by
which they come in an untender world.

if only i could love like that

But for you who revere my name,
the sun of righteousness will rise with
healing in its wings. And you will go out and leap
like calves released from the stall.

MALACHI 4:2

We can have no joy until the rule of love prevails.

JOHN CHRYSOSTOM (AD 347–407)

But with those eyes so much purer than mine,
He'd keep on gazing at me
with a look that reserved for me alone
all his sweet and shaggy life,
always near me, never troubling me,
and asking nothing.

PABLO NERUDA
A DOG HAS DIED

OREO BOUNCED WHEN SHE RAN. With her nose low to the ground, the rest of her seemed to be forced upward as if by springs, her rear end rising and falling in happy cadence, as if loping about could have no other emotion. Life had no weight at all. The activity that engaged the front of her was as impassioned as the back of her seemed indifferent, oblivious. She did all this with a look of mindless delight. But it was more natural than that. For her, it was the normal business of living. She made exploration and wonder look fun, as if that's how nature intended it to look. Pure joy with all its buoyant life fully engaged. *Boing, boing, boing! Happy, happy, happy!*

We thought it might be a Dalmatian thing, but it wasn't as evident in the other two when they came along. It was exclusively an Oreo thing. Savannah and Salem had sufficient bounce and they were "happy dogs," as my wife liked to describe them, but it was of a different intensity and character than Oreo.

When Oreo ran at full speed it was quite a different event. There was nothing quite as fascinating as watching her run. Her body seemed fluid, a creature at one with creation, life doing what it was intended to do, all stops removed. And like everything else she did, she put her full heart into it. It was raw nature on display. I could not help but feel the awe and true miracle of it.

We lived on five acres at the time, so the three dogs could break into a run whenever they pleased, particularly if a rabbit or a squirrel was the object of interest. "Grace" is the applicable word—grace and deep desire. As close as the dogs were to us, as much as they inhabited our private spaces, it was moments like this, watching them run, that the mystery became evident. We were as much a mystery to them, I am sure, but the awe was mutual, a thing we shared that suspended beautifully between us, a joint fascination that love prospers in.

As energetic as they were, they could also be as lazy as dirt. They put as much into their naps as they did anything else.

Though the three of them shared certain breed characteristics, the bounce was pretty much Oreo's. It was reserved for an easier pace, a pace more agreeable with the beat of life: the lope. That is the pace they all made: the lope. Groovin' to the lazy ooze of time. Something else to envy about them. *The lope the lope the lope...*

We attributed everything to that bounce as if it were the essence of what made Oreo *Oreo*. The attachments she made among us were immediate, and they too were happy, springy. Her personality had bounce. Her love had bounce, as love should. There was a bright mischief in her eyes, a thing the other two never seemed to develop with as much verve and pure rascal fun as she did. Maybe we were wiser by the time they came along. Maybe her alpha standing gave her all the consent she needed to be her ultimate self, all restraints undone, all embargoes lifted. Maybe it was just her way. She approached life as if it were truly interesting. It is hard not to attribute this condition to love, which seemed to be her true master.

cheese ball

The one thing Oreo could not do was hide her guilt when she had misbehaved. She knew her crimes and had little cunning in covering them up. She knew us well enough to know what pleased and what didn't please us. And though she always wanted to please, she had lapses. Her devotion was strong, and it remains book worthy, but she was nonetheless an enterprising dog. A great dog, a loving dog, a warm, friendly, devoted dog, but when something was amiss or at the first sign of mischief, she was the usual suspect.

Later Salem followed her lead in household antics, but he didn't have the savvy for it that she did. Then there was Savannah at my feet, always at my feet—warm, rapt Savannah, hardly letting me out of her sight; obedient, fawning, soft Magdalene Savannah, protective, somewhat needier than the others, but beautiful, dedicated, intensely charming Savannah. Her need for me outweighed her need for mischief. More than the other two, she would quiet her instincts for the chance to be near me. Savannah and Oreo were two quite different girls.

One evening we were expecting company for dinner, maybe a week or so before Christmas. Our house was festive with the season, complete with that candlelit mysticism only Christmas can seem to make. All three of the dogs had bells attached to their collars. We could hear them all over the house as they loped about. They didn't seem to mind the small indignity. They figured we liked it.

Benita had worked diligently preparing dinner. It was so long ago, I can't remember what we had that night, but I know it included appetizers, one of which was a large, round, decorative cheese ball. It was about the size of a softball or a large grapefruit. Benita went to a lot of trouble to get it just right: the color, the shape, the texture, the appeal. It had the look of a large Christmas ornament. It was coated with crushed walnuts and other curiosities, some red, some green. The crackers were carefully arranged and cascaded in a complete circle around its base. I almost didn't want to eat it.

But the spell was broken when I heard Benita calling Oreo's name in a loud, exasperated voice. I recognized the tone. It wasn't pretty. Plunder never is. Company had not yet arrived. Benita had stepped out of the kitchen to tend to something at some other part of the house, and in a lapse of judgment Oreo saw her opportunity and took it. She may have been spying, a form of canine stake-out from the side, as she was known to do, waiting for just the right moment of pounce and grab, stealing about, as hush as death. A sudden attack with kamikaze boldness—*a date that will live in infamy*. I can see her now, her eyes on the spoil, her front paws on the table, inching her way forward, making siege upon the unsuspecting cheese ball in sidewise jabs.

Whether she consumed the entire thing in one take (which is my guess) or took her time and savored the moment's ecstasy, the one she knew would have a price, that bliss-filled solitude that predator enjoys over prey is hard to know except by guesswork.

Benita didn't notice the offense when she first returned to the dining room, but when she saw a trail of crumbs and an empty plate with a smear of green, she knew intuitively who the culprit was. Not a difficult bit of detection work either. Other than the swelling of her tummy, the small bits of cheese and walnuts around her mouth, and the odd green stains against her white coat, her actions gave her away. They always did. The dog walked with extreme caution around Benita even before she was found out. The bounce had receded. There was an overall suspicious droop, even in the sound of her bell. Benita knew the look, the slink, the dread in her steps. Something was up. It was also in Oreo's eyes. *Gotcha!*

The other two just didn't have the taste for exploit that she did.

When company came that night, the evidence had been swept clean. There was no cheese ball. There were just a few guests, a great dinner of traditional Christmas fare, and one bloated dog making light and obsequious steps around us, particularly around Benita.

The dog courted her favor for quite some time after that. She even made little cries at times. She probably figured that if she didn't hold a grudge, why should Benita? The worst thing for a dog, particularly that dog, was to be out of favor, to hear impatience or worse in our voices. She could easily read our expressions. She knew us that well. I can't remember any table offenses after that. And as the dog expected, Benita forgave the offense.

The bounce returned. But that's what bounce does.

a love-healthy heart

Of the three dogs, Oreo was observably the most independent. Blame it on her being the first, perhaps, and the two or so years she had us all to herself. But she was that way the first day we met her, the day we brought her home. Her independence was a happy one.

When we first got Oreo we lived in a condominium near Atlanta. There was a large field close by, and one or more of us walked her every day. Adam was nine at the time, and one of his chores was to walk her on occasion. He hated that. Not because he didn't love the dog and not because he had a child's usual aversion to exercise or uninteresting activity. The dog was just too much for him. All we had to do was hand Adam the leash and his usual smile would drop, replaced by the small deflated look of "why me?" Of course the dog was at the front door, steeped in the delirium of anticipation, looking for the moment to bolt into the sun, going through every possible emotion accompanied by squeals of joy. It was pitiful and entertaining at the same time.

Oreo was a large dog; Adam was not a large boy. She was an adventurous dog. She was an explorer. She was literally led around by her nose—her chief sense. And there was the bounce to consider, a thing Adam had little appreciation for at the time. While Adam was a bright, adventurous boy with sufficient bounce of his own, the two of them never quite found the "boy and his dog" resonance.

> Love has bounce. Love should have bounce. I doubt that we can call it love if it doesn't have bounce. It should come with springs.

Adam was obedient. He did the chore. But I think she just wore him out. After a few times of watching his hopeless attempts to corral her, the miles of fruitless chase, of trying to regain her leash after she bolted, of being dragged for short distances, suffering mouthfuls of grass or dirt, we decided that walking her was a mom and dad thing.

• • • • • • • • • • • • • • • • • • • •

*I remember preaching once to Savannah. She loved the sound
of my voice, the rise and fall of emotion, the dynamic shifts,
the lyrical spew, but in the end all I got was a long groan and
a side-to-side shift of her body just before she dozed off.*

• • • • • • • • • • • • • • • • • • • •

Love has bounce. Love should have bounce. I doubt that we can
call it love if it doesn't have bounce. It should come with springs. A
love-healthy heart has elasticity. It is pliable, malleable, supple. It has
sufficient recoverability and resilience, as well as relentless resolve.

We too easily understand the image of the hardened heart, the
bounce-deprived heart, the impenetrable, closed, world-weary heart,
the inflexible, secluded heart, the heart fitted with elaborate defenses—
mine fields and trip wires. Regardless of degree, it is a sad condition.

Many suffer this isolation and are not even aware of it. Usually it
is self-imposed. In the face of an unbearable loneliness, we have convinced ourselves that exposure makes us cold, that vulnerability is at
best unwise, that being alone is better than being hurt. These and
other arguments feed the myth.

Authentic love has stores of rebound within it, stores of bounceback
and return. According to the Oxford English Dictionary, "bounceback" means "rapid recovery; a rebound; resilience." Remembering
Adam, I suppose love has sufficient tug as well. We do what we can
to hold on because it is overpowering. Love has life within it that is
bigger than us. It has better plans and greater resolve. We can find
ourselves facedown in the dirt. We can be jerked around helplessly if
we're not sure of what we're doing or why we might be doing it, or if
our submission is questionable.

bruises, bumps, and the dream of community

Love demands intimacy, and intimacy can result in bruises and bumps.
This makes bounce a good thing. Look at the life of Jesus, or his
prophet John the Baptist; look at Paul or anyone in Scripture who
risked everything, as most of them did. The harder they loved, the

deeper and bluer the wound, the more certain the death appointed them. None were exempt.

Awe surrounds love for these very reasons. It should never be entered into lightly. Keats said, "Love is not a plaything."[1] Keats was right.

Mount Sinai was alive with the presence of God. It shook with violence. God descended in the cloud and met with man on its heights. Is this not what love does? Does it not meet with man in an elevated place? Does it not shake him to his foundations? The answer is a thorough *yes*.

Love can be painfully intrusive at times. Invasive. After all, it seeks possession of the whole. Love has rights to the whole, to the all-or-nothing absolute. It is the very nature of God to possess *the whole*. Why would we give him anything less? Why should he ask anything less from us? Why should a husband or a wife settle for anything less from each other? The heart was equipped for this type of possession, for this knowledge to exist between two individuals.

And still we so often hoard ourselves. We keep a small portion back, not realizing that if we hold back at all, we hold back all.

Intimacy might be defined as the mutual sharing of otherwise private space, a surrendering of one's solitude. Love is not love without it. There is a "letting in" that happens, a voiceless entreaty of "Welcome to my inner space. I avail myself to you." It draws me into a type of living unity with another person, one as confused, as indifferent, as lovely, as wanting, as complaining, and as curious as I am. The OED defines "intimate" as "pertaining to the inmost thoughts or feelings; proceeding from, concerning, or affecting one's inmost self; closely personal." It is not difficult to see why intimacy is such a fearful enterprise and why we try so hard to protect ourselves from its scrutiny.

Authentic love meddles with us thoroughly, deliberately, and with precision. It won't leave us alone. It means giving something up, surrendering whatever is asked. But love also changes the way we perceive. It alters and sanctifies our perception of others, even as it alters and sanctifies the way we perceive ourselves. This tends to make surrender not only possible, but preferable. Like Bernard, we jettison the old life, the old perceptions, for a truer one.

To follow the narrative from Genesis, woman was taken out of the man in a time of deep slumber. He awoke as one wakes from a dream and there she was. We can only imagine how deep this dream of union was, in a sense *his dream of community*. Woman was drawn from the heart of this dream. I am speaking, of course, in metaphor, but if you look close enough, the image is rather conspicuous, as if God is trying to tell us something about our deeper nature as well as the nature of union with each other and with him.

A kind of "waking" always precedes union and nakedness.

After all the good God had accomplished, man's loneliness was the first mention of something that was "not good."[2] An amendment of creation was necessary. Man had access and private audience with God, but even God conceded that something was unfinished. After all, God lives in a kind of community of his own, an agreement of three in one. We were fashioned as a likeness, a reflection, but with a difference. God alone is complete in himself. This is where the likeness ends. For the man, being a likeness of God, community was necessary, and indeed community was found *in* him. But it was also separate from him, outside him.

It was an easy fix.

God drew community out of the man. From the stuff of man's desiring he fashioned the woman. He drew union from inside him. The man's loneliness had a shape. It had a form like his but not like his. It was of his kind but unlike him. It reflected the beauty of the garden, a beauty that was in man from the beginning, a hint of God. She was a glory to him, even as nakedness was a glory to them. She was a creature of the garden. She was and remains Eden to the man.

Marriage is an image of return, of *re*union, of the separated unseparating, a wholeness, a completing, an image more like God than the man alone. The image clarifies, indeed, lives and replicates itself.

They walked and lived in a type of revelation, an uncovering, remembering that everything in the garden was replete with meaning. Intimacy was as bright and prophetic as anything in Eden. As was man's nakedness. God was pleased in what he had done. His pleasure sustained the garden in which they lived. It had physical and mystical presence, as it still does. Creation was complete. The garden was complete. God's pleasure, as alive and present as himself, was complete. Eden was home to man.

We have distanced ourselves from our beginnings. I opened my window last night and heard coyotes howl in the distance. It was lonesome in a way I cannot explain. It saddens me to think how removed we are from nature, how our dependencies have changed, and how exiled we have become from ourselves.

Our craving is a profound one. A homesickness there is little cure for. Man's deep memory is suffused with the perfume of his origins.

* *

For I have learned
To look on nature, not as in the hour
Of thoughtless youth; but hearing oftentimes
The still, sad music of humanity...

And I have felt
A presence that disturbs me with the joy
Of elevated thoughts; a sense sublime
Of something far more deeply interfused,
Whose dwelling is the light of setting suns,
And the round ocean and the living air,
And the blue sky, and in the mind of man;
A motion and a spirit, that impels
All thinking things, all objects of all thought,
And rolls through all things.

WILLIAM WORDSWORTH
COMPOSED NEAR TINTERN ABBEY, 1798

* *

This presence does disturb. It is sad to think that I was designed to live in the pleasure of God, to live in union with him, to live in agreement with nature itself, and yet deny myself this birthright. The heart was equipped to understand what "forever" means. Now that same "forever" is consigned to poems and Hallmark cards because we have become strangers to it.

You and I were designed to live and prosper in community. We were made for the *agape* life, a life of love, a conditionless, raw, and uncivilized love. We were designed to live a surrendered life, a selfless life that actualizes self, a life of sacrifice that seems anything but sacrificial, a life of fulfillment, of irrevocable joy, deathless joy, outrageous and irresistible, a life of deep contentment, imperturbable, immovable, a life we may say is complete, holy according to its design.

"Agape" [αγαπε, Greek. *ag-ah'-pay*] means "love." In verb form, it is the same word Jesus used when he commanded us to "love each other"[3] and Paul when he wrote 1 Corinthians 13. My dogs had no sense for translation, but they understood the word fairly well—and the life it asked of them.

Love is not convenient. It meddles. It intrudes. It is an affront to my alienation. It is a threat to my isolation. It costs too much, and the light is always on.

> O LORD, you have searched me and you know me. You know when I sit and when I rise; you perceive my thoughts from afar. You discern my going out and my lying down; you are familiar with all my ways.
>
> Before a word is on my tongue you know it completely, O LORD. You hem me in—behind and before; you have laid your hand upon me. Such knowledge is too wonderful for me, too lofty for me to attain. Where can I go from your Spirit? Where can I flee from your presence?
>
> If I go up to the heavens, you are there; if I make my bed in the depths, you are there. If I rise on the wings of the dawn, if I settle on the far side of the sea, even there your hand will guide me, your right hand will hold me fast. If I say, "Surely the darkness will hide me and the light become night around me," even the darkness will not be dark to you; the night will shine like the day, for darkness is as light to you.
>
> For you created my inmost being; you knit me together in my mother's womb. I praise you because I am fearfully and wonderfully made; your works are wonderful, I know that full well. My frame was not hidden from you when I was made in the secret place. When I was woven together in the

depths of the earth, your eyes saw my unformed body. All the days ordained for me were written in your book before one of them came to be.

—PSALM 139:1-16

In the devoted life, this intrusiveness is meant as a comfort. There is redemption in it: God keeping his end of the bargain. He desires the whole, not part, for there really is no part. There is only the whole of life. The psalmist doesn't stop until his revelation turns to prayer.

Search me, O God, and know my heart; test me and know my anxious thoughts. See if there is any offensive way in me, and lead me in the way everlasting.

—PSALM 139:23-24

heavy meddle

Everything Jesus did was intimate. His exchanges with Pilate were no less intimate than his exchanges with the woman at the well or with Peter on the night he was betrayed. His rebukes were intimate. Turning over the tables of the moneychangers[4] was as much an act of intimacy, an act of severe love, as weeping at the tomb of Lazarus or having his feet bathed with the tears of the Magdalene.[5]

Everything love does is intimate—every action it takes. Because of this, it was impossible to maintain a middle distance from Jesus. People either loved him or hated him. And nothing has really changed. As we saw in chapter 3, there is no middle way, no half measures. You are either in or out. You are either gathering or scattering.[6] Nothing is passive. Your *no* is as alive and active as your *yes*, and a simple *yes* or *no* is sufficient only because that is all there is. Love provides no gray, not the slightest loophole to obscure its right to the whole. It is an incredibly simple economy. The accounting is accurate, and nothing is wasted. The simple but incredibly clear economy of love.

Love demands a nakedness, that a kind of revelation prosper between two individuals. "I am open to scrutiny. My door is unlocked. My heart—with all its flaws, with all its mystery, all its lovely unknown—and my faith with all its uncertainties are an open book. There is complement for you here, agreement, an answer to your own riddle. In love I am not afraid, even if you fail me, if you give me over to my tormentors."

All of us have been hurt by someone close to us. It is a sad but inevitable condition of life. Once wounded, we often retreat behind a protective covering. Sometimes the strategy is simple and conspicuous; sometimes subtle and very clever. Either way the bounce recedes. The once bright smile begins to dull. Something within us, once in bloom closes up and contracts. The plates of our armor thicken. Memory logs the complaint rather sharply, and we enter into the next relationship cautiously, circumspectly, if at all. We go in ankle deep. Engagement is at best an illusion, a fiction, short-lived, and without substance. The mind occupies itself with strategies. The heart entangles itself in coils and webbing. This is an odd custom indeed, but an incredibly common one.

* *

*The Latin root from where we get our English word
"person" is "persona," which means "mask."*

* *

Why am I afraid to allow someone close access to me? What might someone read in me that I don't want them to read? Why do I fear judgment? Why do I prefer opacity to transparency? Why is vulnerability so unwise? Why do I invent disguises to hide myself? What am I afraid of? Why am I asking questions like these?

Even as I write this, I am at a safe distance from you. This very moment you are somewhere in the future. Once this book is in your hands you may get a sense of me as you read. You may find me warm, passionate, eager. You may find me annoying, pretentious, hiding my insecurity in lyrical speech. Then there is my neediness to consider, my hope that you will like me.

Perhaps there is a resonance between us already, a frequency that unites us. Maybe you actually like Shakespeare. Maybe you are still waiting for the payoff and are willing to stall your impatience until you feel I actually say something. Maybe we share similar convictions. Maybe there is one line you particularly like. Or one you hate. Maybe you would like nothing better than to throw something at me.

In spite of how conversational I wish to be, you are still reading this at a distance. I have no specific image of you, only a vague idea of a single reader.

Every author hopes someone will read his words with interest, make judgments, laugh, cry, engage, anticipate, and indeed, this is a type of intimacy. But as you read, I am sitting somewhere else in time. There is a divide between you and me. Degrees of separation. The distance insulates me. It protects me like a barrier or like armor. This book, like any book, is a stage, a remote island.

You will come to know me as words permit. Sadly, it is what we have.

Talking about intimacy is easy. *Being* intimate is another thing altogether. Religion has become a workable substitute for it. Religion is easy. It doesn't ask that much of you and me. By rote or habit I can do what is required. I can follow the canons, recite the creeds, and so on. But authentic Christianity is an active engagement of the heart, love without restraints, adventurous, detailed, a bit uncivilized. In truth, there is little else beyond that.

Community is the imperative not by suggestion but by command.

reason only interferes—heart over mind

So what is keeping me from doing it right? Distractions come in many forms. *Thinking* is one of them. The mind of man possesses boundless capacity, but as busy as it is, as great a machine as it has proven to be, with as much swiftness and precision as the wheels can spin, it can be its worst enemy in matters of the heart.

Thinking is perhaps the greatest impediment to love. Love and logic are incompatible. We cannot talk ourselves into love nor can we reason it away. Reason only interferes. Love engages a completely different part of us, an altogether different precinct, the one closer to divinity, closer to our origins.

There was a time when heart and mind were at peace one with the other, when they lived in absolute agreement, in a time when the heart had preeminence over mind, when man understood his own heart, when there was no distance between him and his origins, when the heart held the seat of power. The mind of man was free to operate at full capacity because it was under dominion. Love was sovereign. The heart was not yet a thing to be redeemed.

· · · · · · · · · · · · · · · · · · ·

*To say the truth, reason and love keep
little company together now-a-days.*

WILLIAM SHAKESPEARE
A MIDSUMMER NIGHT'S DREAM

· · · · · · · · · · · · · · · · · · ·

Intimacy is mindless. Warmth and touch need no thought. Love engages something higher than intellect. Intellect is no more efficient in love than it is in understanding God. Intellectual ascent to God just doesn't work. It is the same in love. Love did not begin with the mind and does little commerce there. It is charged with way too much divinity. Love is much too unreasonable to give any satisfaction of mind.

An accomplished musician who has rehearsed a piece of music until she knows it intimately or "by heart," arrives at a place where she no longer has to think about it. Memory infuses the fingers, the emotions outside the mechanics of thought. Maybe that is why they call it "play" in the first place. Who knows? Only the rules of intimacy apply. Unity is engaged—unity between her and her instrument and between her and her audience. It is outside explanation, outside thought. The more complete her inward unity, the more completely she can unite with others. A formidable rule.

There is a kind of nakedness involved as well. A type of waking, a type of love. Many times a piece of music, poetry, even a passage of Scripture is executed with such grace and transparency it has moved me so deeply as to lay part of me open to the elements. A *"killing me softly"* kind of thing. This happened to me once in a restaurant in

Florida. A young man was playing violin, taking requests. It was summer. He was a Julliard student and played beautifully. I asked him if he would play a song. I couldn't remember the name of the song so I hummed part of it. He began to play. The song was Beethoven's *Pathetique*. A sad, sweet melody that the young man executed with uncommon tenderness. Taken totally off guard, and in the middle of a busy restaurant during lunch on a Sunday afternoon, I wept. And wept. Not loud and not hard, but sufficiently, thoroughly. I was useless. I wanted it to stop but didn't want it to stop at the same time.

> Love engages a completely different part of us, an altogether different precinct, the one closer to divinity, closer yet to our origins.

An actor who has memorized his lines can put his heart into it because he no longer has to work his thoughts to retain it. The words belong to him. He can engage the proper emotion. He can *become* the part. Again, this is outside thinking.

In the movie *Love Affair*, Warren Beatty plays a retired star athlete who now announces games. When asked in an interview about the technique of star quarterbacks, he says, "The great ones don't think." The dynamic is the same. Something closer than thought engages, something richer, deeper, purer, more primal than mind. The mind is under new government. The judgments it makes are under a new authority.

And the bounce returns. As free of thought as it was with Oreo, it is possible to liberate the bounce between you and the life around you. If love is a mindless proposition, and it is, if it engages heart over mind, and it does, fear is a nonissue, an alien, a square among round parts.

okay, i left out a detail

By the way, we also had a cat. Okay, I left out a detail. Here we are, almost at the finale and he confesses. You can hardly hold it against me. This is about dogs, right? But to be fair, I will tell the whole story.

When Shad was six, we got him a calico kitten Benita found

somewhere. Who knows where? A strip mall, a garage sale, neighbors. This was mommy's turf. Shad had asked for a kitten, something that could be his, that might be more manageable for his size. The dogs were his, of course, but they were communal property. They belonged to everybody. Good parents that we were, we complied.

Unfortunately, the kitten had a short life.

No, it had nothing to do with the dogs. They were kind, gentle, and hardly had time to get to know the little stranger. It was an accident, a tragic one for the kitten, and I suppose for Shad too, for all of us.

It had only been a few weeks, and yet Shad grieved over the loss. We even gave it a proper burial with all rites and funerary courtesies. A prayer, a moment of silence, a cross Shad made out of two sticks and Scotch tape. The cat had a name, after all. Naming changes things. There is a degree of intimacy involved—initiation, identification, belonging. Anyway, its four white boots against a mottle of calico made a nice contrast. I think it would have been a beautiful adult. It is a shame it had such a short life span. We called her Spatz.

I will spare you the details. It was my fault. It was one of those moments that sickens you, an accident I could not prevent or anticipate, but Shad tagged me for it. It became the cloud over my head. We immediately found him another kitten, a solid white one we named… well, I named, Sugar. Another strip mall, a garage sale, a Wal-Mart parking lot. Benita has a gift for these things. Our population now eight.

Anyway, by the time Sugar came along, all three dogs were at full height and speed. Salem and Savannah were not quite adults yet, but they were formidable dogs, much larger than the kitten who, even in adulthood, remained rather small. Wiry. Quiet. Fast. Very smart. Good equipment for a cat among dogs. *A very shrewd David among three slower Goliaths.*

The dogs took to her immediately. Each one of them found their own rhythm with the cat, their own engagement style.

Salem thought she was a toy. He loved to chase her around the house. The two of them would break into a run. She had this way, once we noticed it, of enticing him. Maybe it was a look she gave him or a suggestion of pounce. She loved the play. She would just bolt, and he would bolt after her. At times she even chased him, though I am not sure either one of them were aware that this particular order made any sense.

Oreo got into the fun at times, but usually this was between Salem and Sugar. She would get him all worked up and then find a nice perch somewhere close and watch him torture himself with search. No expression, just this glib feline contentment, this profoundly cat satisfaction, the superiority they seem to be sure of.

Cats.

He caught her once, actually a few times. We all knew the cat let him, out of pity perhaps or just to keep the game interesting, to keep him hoping. Whenever he actually did catch her he was never quite sure what to do with her. He mouthed her softly, gently, almost toothless, and she would bat at him playfully, without claws or malice. He seemed to like the abuse. It was their style of intimacy. They were friends. It was a strange love.

Between Savannah and Sugar, nothing. These two never found any reference between them. Only bristle. Savannah had one obsession—me. Even the cat knew it. And she was a threat. Loyalties were at stake perhaps. Who knows? That slight uncertainty that dogs always suffer from a cat made Savannah suspicious. The cat could not resist a good challenge.

Benita always told me Sugar had a thing for me. Though I hardly believed it, many times if I happened to be napping or just lying around, maybe reading, the cat seemed to enjoy lying on my chest. It was like the height of achievement for her. Her stealth was so perfect, so practiced, she was so light and ghostlike, she was on top of me before I even noticed. She would dig into my flesh, as they do, with soft alternating pads, kneading, kneading, purring, left, right, left, right, purring, hypnotizing. I don't understand cats enough to get that.

The best Savannah could do was to stare at the spectacle from a

> No expression, just this glib feline contentment, this profoundly cat satisfaction, the superiority they seemed to be sure of. *Cats.*

short distance away. Anticipating. Jealous. Something accelerating in her blood. Vengeful. Impatient. Tolerant. Well, hardly tolerant. She ran Sugar off more than a few times when she found her performing the old soft shoe on my chest. Savannah's chase had something else in it, something Salem's did not have and the cat did not like.

> Savannah and Sugar respected each other, I suppose, but there was no engagement between them at all. Just cold recognition, the antagonism of charmed rivals.

Savannah and Sugar respected each other, I suppose, but there was no engagement between them at all. Just cold recognition. The antagonism of charmed rivals.

Oreo and Sugar, however, became the best of friends. Of course they did. Oreo was like that. We found them asleep together often. All rules, all precedents between the species were rewritten with this pair. Oreo had that kind of generosity and warmth about her. Her love was big enough to disperse widely, liberally.

Oreo became mom to this little apparition when she first arrived. She had none of the classic animal prejudices. On the rare occasion we found all three dogs asleep with Sugar nested among them.

I said Savannah was the inspiration for this book, and I will stick to that. She had the most intense and most conspicuous love for her master. All the major elements were there to make the metaphor complete. But when I think about it now, I am convinced that Oreo's devotion was just as strong, just as complete. And hers was the very image of lightness, a precocious, joyful, liberated, large, and loving spirit, perhaps the largest of them all. She had less need to state it than Savannah did, to drive it as strong.

I think of all of them, Oreo had the right idea. She was the artist in loving. Love was the easiest on her, the most attractive, in some ways the most powerful and yet the lightest, most understated.

the gospel according to the dog

Now that I have introduced Sugar or "the Cat," as she was known at times, and have told you my big secret, I have one more Oreo story to tell, maybe the best of them. It is not a funny story. It will not make you laugh, but I think this tale stands in sharp relief from the other stories in this book, and it too has to do with a cat. Not Sugar this time, but another one, a drifter that came into our yard, a sick, scruffy-looking cat with no name.

Benita discovered her in our garage. It didn't take long to notice the cat was "with child." It also didn't take long to notice that not only was her time near, but that she was weak, slow, suffering some unknown ailment.

It was early on a Monday. Benita made a bed out of a cardboard box, folded a blanket or a towel in it, and made the cat as comfortable as she could. The cat did not resist. She accepted Benita's kindness. She understood the softness in her hands meant something friendly.

The day progressed. The cat did not stir. Benita thought it best to let it sleep. She and I had to prepare for the Bible study that evening as we did every Monday. We kept the dogs away from the cat, to not frighten or upset her in the condition she was in. We did not have to try that hard. They knew a suffering animal when they saw one. It softened among them. They made no fuss. Like so many things with them, it was easy. None of them bothered the cat. Well, with one exception.

With evening approaching, Benita and I were occupied with food and setting up chairs, candles, lighting a good fire, and all the preparations for the evening. All the animals were on their own.

During our Bible study, instead of sitting or sleeping quietly by my side as Oreo always did, as everyone expected her to do, she sat at the back door and made small crying noises, sympathetic noises that were hard to ignore. The sick cat was on the other side of the door.

In an act of trust, Benita eventually opened the door and let Oreo into the garage. The cat didn't move. She was not alarmed. She may have been too weak to care. Or maybe animals have a sense of each other. That was my bet. Either way, there was no noise at all, and no more crying from Oreo.

After some time the suspense became too much. Benita went to check on the pair. She came back into the room a few minutes later, her eyes sparkling, and with a slight smile that resembled amazement, awe. She put her finger to her mouth and asked me to come and see. Quietly. The room quickened with anticipation.

When I went to the door of the garage, I looked in and saw the cat in the makeshift bed. Oreo was coiled around her—maternal, angelic, serene. She flattened the back of the cardboard box with her weight. There was more dog than bed. But her own comfort wasn't the issue.

Even with the familiar faces at the door she did not move or leave the cat. She turned her head once or twice our way and that was all. Her obligation was stronger than either her common joys or the biases of nature. Everyone in the Bible study got a peek at this small *agape* miracle.

Whatever I taught that night became insignificant and receded far into the background. A bigger picture came into view, blinding us with clarity. The dog had the greater gospel to share.

* * * * * * * * * * * * * * * * * * * *

This is the LORD's doing; it is marvellous in our eyes.

PSALM 118:23 KJV

* * * * * * * * * * * * * * * * * * *

* * * * * * * **prayer for the love-healthy heart** * * * * * * * *

Lord, restore the bounce—the happy, daring, joyful springs of life. Touch me with miracle. I want to love like that. Selfless, mindless, without the restrictions of thought and argument, without thought of my own comfort. Put in me a love-healthy heart. Activate it. Make it live. I want to be free of distraction, free of the weights that keep me earthbound. I want to be that feather in the wind. Cleanse my thought life of all its debris, all its misbelief. Make my mind a holy place, a sacred temple. Put agreement between my heart and my mind once again. Teach me to love purely without thought of reward other than the loving itself. That I too might be the warm coil, someone's angel of comfort—sympathetic, selfless, serene.

In Christ, the bigger picture, Christ, my fearlessness, my warmth, my clarity. Amen.

May love give you understanding outside
what you see, what you think, what you feel.

and finally, it was my dogs who taught me to stop and smell, well, everything

They haven't got no noses
They haven't got no noses
And goodness only knowses
The noselessness of Man!

G.K. CHESTERTON
THE FLYING INN

Those who don't feel this Love
pulling them like a river,
those who don't drink dawn
like a cup of spring water
or take in sunset like supper,
those who don't want to change,
let them sleep.

This love is beyond the study of theology,
that old trickery and hypocrisy.
If you want to improve your mind that way,
sleep on.

I've given up on my brain.
I've torn the cloth to shreds
and thrown it away.

If you're not completely naked,
wrap your beautiful robe of words
around you,
and sleep.

RUMI
THIRTEENTH-CENTURY PERSIAN POET AND MYSTIC

WHEN RAISING BOYS, "BUSTLE" IS the adjective that describes life the best. The dogs were great with bustle. They enjoyed the pace, the randomness, the perpetual adolescence of it, the small bright madness it took just to hold all our seams together. To this day we don't mention Oreo's name without small laughter, mixed with a kind of pride. She was all ours. Salem's name doesn't come up without shaking our heads with a smile of light comic disgust mingled with something warm and unforgetting. And then there's Savannah, the lover among them, the hopeless devotee, grown weak under love's great weight, soft and submissive Savannah, the warm coil at my feet.

They deserve the press, and it just proves that love is always young, that it never dies, that love's memory is long and just as deathless, and the lessons it has to teach are always necessary, always alive, never frivolous or small, and they are always right on time.

this deep drink of life

All we had to do was get one of the three leashes off the rack in the kitchen. The sound was enough to generate impatience and desire. *Fellowship, fellowship, fellowship!* Tails wagging in a fever pitch, *allegro.* Breath and pulse accelerating. *Joy, joy, joy!*

Walking the dogs was a David or Benita event. Many times we walked them together at the end of the day. It was a time we had with them and with ourselves. My wife and I still hold hands in church, and it was the same when we walked the dogs. Hand to hand, hand to leash, leash to dog, we were all connected, all drifting together in no particular direction for no particular purpose, under no obligation to time or other restraints.

Occasionally we attempted taking all three of them, but that was a little more work than we had energy for after a long day. The idea was leisure, the great littleness of a walk. The talk was small, the time spent together restorative, and the medicine we made together kept life interesting and love flirtatious.

● ● ● ● ● ● ● ● ● ● ● ● ● ● ● ● ● ●

In this ability to seize the world anew at every
moment, the dog is our superior.

JEFFREY MASSON
DOGS NEVER LIE ABOUT LOVE

● ● ● ● ● ● ● ● ● ● ● ● ● ● ● ● ● ●

They loved the walk. They had us to themselves, separate and alone. The attention could be focused, and there is the excitement of venturing into territory beyond our little camp.

When it was time to take a walk, it was first come, first serve. Benita would take one dog, I would take another. There were times we took only one dog between us. Those were the best of times. One dog is manageable. It is peaceful, and the appreciation is conspicuous. One dog behaves differently than two or three. She has better manners. She doesn't have to share anything, and her instincts are not aggravated by the tribe.

We walked in shifts if the demands were pressing, if one of them felt left out, which they did often. But whether we took one dog or all of them, there was one thing we could never avoid. The street we lived on was rather isolated. Houses were spaced at a considerable distance, and a wood stretched maybe 300 feet or more directly across from us. This was the stretch of road we walked every day. It was a road to temptation.

The nose, that cold damp gate of sense, that chief negotiator of life, made demands, irresistible demands, and with all authority. Against all hope, the calm quiet walk was overturned by sudden bursts of lunge and desire.

"Oh! Oh! Oh! What is that? That is rich! Rich! *Just look! That mysterious heap just lying there—so fragrant, so delicate, so…so unattended, so very mine! And this flower, this weed, this drooping thing! You don't know what you're missing! Smell, smell,* smell! *Put your nose into it! O, the happiness! Isn't life great!"*

And so on and so on the song goes.

Lunge, lunge!

Of course, this is the book version. If you were actually there, you

would know better. They didn't bother with punctuation or even something as conventional as space between words. It was more like:

> ohohohwhatisthatthatisrichrichjustlookthatmysterious
> heapjustlyingtheresofragrantsodelicatesosounattendedsovery
> mineandthisflowerthisweedthisdroopingthingyoudontknow
> whatyouremissingsmellsmellsmellputyournoseintoitothe
> happinessisntlifegreat

 We were busy meeting the challenge, trying to regain control. The
dogs were about the business of being themselves. Realizing their desire
to indulge the moment was stronger than our ability to recapture command, many times we simply stopped, and with a sigh of resignation,
let them have their way. We stood idly by, impatient, anxious to move
on, not quite as fascinated as they were.

And we missed the whole point.

Benita and I, during those years, had become busy with life. We
didn't notice the speed by which our wheels were turning. Life, as it
can, took on an unnatural pace. It was easy to miss things. I remember
my dad, for instance. He was retired by then, just into his seventies,
and getting older right before my eyes. We didn't know he was sick.
His heart was weak and getting weaker. I was too aloof, too detached
to make much of it, too self-absorbed to empathize or to stop long
enough to fully engage.

He died January 2001. I was alone with him at the time. I laid my
hand on his heart and felt its last beat. And as moving as that might
sound, as noble as I felt in the awkward moment, I can't remember
allowing myself to close the distance between us while he was alive. The
pace I kept didn't allow for too much small talk or idle engagement.

It wasn't quite as bad as it sounds. He was a good father; I was a
good son. We had our intimate moments. Or I should say as intimate
as we would allow ourselves. We were both afraid, and neither of us
knew why. It is an old theme, and it is usually generations deep. But
it could have been better. Love was not allowed its full reach.

Now that I think about it, my dad got closer to the dogs and the
dogs enjoyed his company once he retired, once life took on a slower
pace. But this is knowledge that comes by reflection and aftershock,

like a sudden blink of insight that comes with a small regret of loss you can't explain or don't wish to explain.

Truth is, I just wasn't paying close enough attention. It wasn't complicated. Love simply could not entrust itself to me. I wasn't all there. There was so much of *me* to contend with, so much of *me* in my own way. I knew what love asked. I was aware that surrender was necessary, but my surrender was not surrender as much as it was the talk of surrender, the image of surrender.

> I was saved, but
> I was unaware
> that redemption
> was bigger, wider,
> longer, and more
> unstoppable than
> I first imagined.

I was saved, but I was unaware that redemption was bigger, wider, longer, and more unstoppable than I imagined it to be. And here is this dog, dragging me over to this dead heap of vegetation by the side of the road, this lump with no name, taking deep drafts of it as if the secret of life were contained in that one desperate intake of smelly air. I say it that way now because perhaps Salem was right. In all his romp and bustle, he had the goods, and I was too distracted to translate his actions into wisdom.

Perhaps the secret of life *was* in that smell. All I felt at the time was mild irritation. The dog and I both had our noses in the air, but for different reasons. I stood there and waited until some meter in him ran out, until something saturated and went quiet. My impatience was senseless. Where was I going on our walk? Was there a destination? Was there some deadline to get there? It seemed rather silly to the dog.

Salem knew love was not in the destination. He knew it wasn't even in the journey, as I had always believed. It was in the moment. Each one counted. He owned each one of them. He made the most of them. They were not unlike the front gate, his plaything, in and out of which he could come and go as he pleased. He possessed each moment fully, squeezing out of each of them a kind of nectar, a sweetness that nature provides for those who really pay attention. Time was his because he paid so little attention to it.

Salem was simply obeying nature, following his nose wherever bliss was to lead him, to some anticipated ecstasy just steps away. He had more of a share of eternity in the moment than I was willing to allow myself.

I know this sounds strange, but if you consider living at capacity as being paradise revisited, the dog was enjoying it to the full. I was outside, not even conscious of its existence, having convinced myself that if man thought his way out of Eden, surely he can somehow think his way back in.

It doesn't work that way.

I wanted to get on with the walk. Busy, busy, busy. Stupid, stupid, stupid.

I was preoccupied. My mind was fully engaged, but elsewhere. My heart was absent. I was no less than an automaton. The closest thing to me with a heart was one spotted dog. He pushed it right up front. He always did.

• • • • • • • • • • • • • • • • • • • •

To walk with a dog is to enter the world of the
immediate. Our dog stares up into a tree, watching
a squirrel—she is there and nowhere else.
JEFFREY MASSON
DOGS NEVER LIE ABOUT LOVE

• • • • • • • • • • • • • • • • • • • •

Maybe Salem wanted to share his good fortune, maybe not. I suspect he did. He hoarded bones from the others. He hoarded his bed once he was settled in it—or at least he didn't budge when one of the other two lay next to him. But as all of them were, he was generous, liberal. He had no real possessions and no desire to spend his brief life seeking after them. He suffered no illusions. Had I wanted his bone, he would have surrendered it to me. But in those moments of scent, something quite determined rose up in him, something he couldn't help, something bigger than obedience or protocol. He couldn't resist the urges that took possession of him through the tireless industry of his nose.

Being the witless Timmy to his wise and far-seeing Lassie, Salem was trying to tell me something. In all the heave and fury of his leash and with colorful exclamation, if not a hint of warning, he was saying, *"Stop! Don't you get it yet? At least slow down! If you're not that thirsty, fine, but let me enjoy this one deep drink of life! There is nothing more important than this. Here we are, now, exclusive of all other places, all other times. Can we enjoy this for what it is? Look what I have found! Look at this! Can you smell that? How can you be so complacent, so removed, so distant at a moment like this?"*

> He possessed each moment fully, squeezing out of each of them a kind of nectar, a sweetness that nature provides for those who really pay attention.

His English was quite good. He almost trembled with delight.

What looked like a waste of time to me was treasure and spoil to him. All time and eternity mingled together for him in that one feast of smell. Paradise was accessible. He could indulge his deepest senses with no restraint. Our dogs could pursue bliss with as much thought as we might give to a sip of tea in the afternoon. Time always conferred on them its freshness, its first flourish. They were the masters of it. Time had no claim on them. It held no contracts or indenture.

If it is true that dogs have mastery over time (and only because it is a trifle to them, something they can live without), then it is just as true that time has mastery over the rest of us. We draft words like "tyranny" to describe our relationship to time. Deadlines are real. The eight hours allotted to me are not the ten I need. I become lined and wrinkled, bent and hardened by time. So what does the dog have to teach us that might alter this savage course? Simple:

> The feast is closer than we think. Paradise is as available as we truly desire it to be. It is perhaps one sudden lunge away. Maybe we just haven't gotten the scent quite yet. Or we're just not desperate enough.

The other lesson is the obvious one. Reconsider your relationship to time. Like the hostility between mind and heart, so time and eternity still clamor for the soul of man.

The complete man, the man who dares to live at capacity, is the man who lives in the balance between the two, in that middle place, the lovely in-between. He is the man who is aware of time, but chooses eternity instead. He understands the compatibility between the two. Therefore, time is no longer the tyrant, but the friend.

One master for life, that is the rule.

The dog never lost her paradise. She knows right where it is. It is suspended in the next smell, in the next soft nap in the sun, in the walk with her best friend in the afternoon, and on the hillside doing absolutely nothing. Engaging divinity among the ordinary. I was merely attempting life when it was intended to be enjoyed.

the inspired life

My dogs were outrageously enthusiastic. They were always up, always *on*. They were always happy, always willing. They could never turn us down. The pitch was always high. They didn't know the difference between the grand and the commonplace. To them everything was grand—particularly the commonplace. They always came at life with a full heart. Fascination was commonplace.

Perhaps more than anything else it might be, the devoted life is an *inspired* life. Inspiration was, from our origins, a common element of human existence. Literally the breath of God, it not only gave life to man, but he could take it in by deep drafts.[1] It governed his thought life. Fascination was easy. Inspiration was a way of life. The grand was commonplace. Both body and brain went at it with all their might, and it did not weary him. He did not yet labor, though he put his whole heart into all he did. He knew no other way. He had full possession of his heart. He lived comfortably with awe. His senses were elevated: physical, spiritual, and those we have forgotten.

The devoted life gives us a way back. In our devaluation of para-dise we reassigned inspiration, put it out of our direct reach. The devoted life is the means by which we may be trusted with it again, the means by which the extraordinary remains extraordinary, there is just more of it.

We can live in agreement with our origins again. Worship and life can mingle purely and become indistinguishable, bringing us into a renewed state of awareness. Our perceptions are washed clean. Our judgments are purified, all the waste removed, all former bias. Experience is transformed into wisdom—the inspired kind of wisdom that comes with the seal and imprimatur of God—life-giving, life-enhancing, life-enlarging:

> As his anointing teaches you about all things and as that anointing is real, not counterfeit—just as it has taught you, remain in him.
>
> —1 JOHN 2:27

We perceive and judge by way of inspired vision. We speak by inspiration. We sense and understand by inspiration. We become the true artists, the mystics, the healers, the poets, bringing the beauty of God into the ordinary—into our conversations, into our private meditations, into our e-mails, into our jobs and our to-do lists, into anyplace we have expression and presence. What thoughts we have are washed clean of mortality.

Life is elevated. Language is elevated. Heart and mind are united once again, the long divorce over. Redemption, far from being an isolated event, distills into each moment, slowing time itself. How is this possible? The devoted life makes this possible. Being your truest self makes this possible, by conforming to that which you were created to be.

rhapsody

The language of romance is always lyrical. It is unavoidable. Inspiration is at work—movement in the heart that often demands a reckoning in words. Just as often it does not, for some things have no speech, though the silence is never barren. God is just as alive, just as active, just as immediate, and just as present in silence as in speech.

Simple words come together in simple constructions and cannot help but sing with an undeniable poetry. The greatest poetry is the simplest. Love gives the plainest speech a touch of miracle. There is no finer lyric than "I love you." Or the great opera of a kiss.

The same can be said of the language of Scripture. From cover to cover it must sing or be silent. Each page laments, rejoices, loves, cries, exults, warns, rages, redeems, instructs. Read these words to yourself slowly:

> By the rivers of Babylon we sat and wept when we remembered Zion. There on the poplars we hung our harps, for there our captors asked us for songs, our tormentors demanded songs of joy; they said, "Sing us one of the songs of Zion!" How can we sing the songs of the LORD while in a foreign land? If I forget you, O Jerusalem, may my right hand forget [its skill]. May my tongue cling to the roof of my mouth if I do not remember you, if I do not consider Jerusalem my highest joy.
>
> —PSALM 137:1-6 *(BRACKETS IN ORIGINAL)*

The verses weep and yet sweetly, as one who longs for home. The Scriptures are thick with the ooze of romance, the sweet plaintive voice of a love song that suspends between the lover and the beloved, between heaven and earth. Some of the music of Scripture is more evident than others, like the rich parallel structure of Ecclesiastes 3, whose cadences are like drum taps. The voice of "The Preacher" is a poet's voice:[2]

> There is a time for everything,
>> and a season for every activity under heaven:
>>> a time to be born and a time to die,
>>> a time to plant and a time to uproot,
>>> a time to kill and a time to heal,
>>> a time to tear down and a time to build,
>>> a time to weep and a time to laugh,
>>> a time to mourn and a time to dance,
>>> a time to scatter stones and a time to gather them,
>>> a time to embrace and a time to refrain,
>>> a time to search and a time to give up,
>>> a time to keep and a time to throw away,
>>> a time to tear and a time to mend,
>>> a time to be silent and a time to speak,

a time to love and a time to hate,
a time for war and a time for peace.
—ECCLESIASTES 3:1-8

The Psalms. The book of Job. The words of Jesus, Paul, and John—passages that represent something way beyond plain speech. And David's "Lament of the Bow." This is how God chose and chooses to speak. A touch of rhapsody appealing to the heart alone, the primary sense, his center of commerce:

Your glory, O Israel, lies slain on your heights.
How the mighty have fallen!
Tell it not in Gath,
proclaim it not in the streets of Ashkelon,
lest the daughters of the Philistines be glad,
    lest the daughters of the uncircumcised rejoice.
O mountains of Gilboa,
    may you have neither dew nor rain,
    nor fields that yield offerings [of grain].
For there the shield of the mighty was defiled,
    the shield of Saul—no longer rubbed with oil.
From the blood of the slain,
    from the flesh of the mighty,
the bow of Jonathan did not turn back,
    the sword of Saul did not return unsatisfied.
Saul and Jonathan—
    in life they were loved and gracious,
    and in death they were not parted.
They were swifter than eagles,
    they were stronger than lions.
O daughters of Israel,
    weep for Saul,
who clothed you in scarlet and finery,
    who adorned your garments with ornaments of gold.
How the mighty have fallen in battle!
    Jonathan lies slain on your heights.
I grieve for you, Jonathan my brother;
    you were very dear to me.

Your love for me was wonderful,
    more wonderful than that of women.
How the mighty have fallen!
The weapons of war have perished!
—2 SAMUEL 1:19-27 *(BRACKETS IN ORIGINAL)*

Scripture keeps itself at a slight remove from us. Slight but sufficient. Giving what it chooses to give, what it may entrust us with, withholding what it must withhold.[3] It is a lifelong courtship. When I first met Benita, though it was love at first sight, possession wasn't immediate. Intimacy and trust were involved, patience and seasoning—both of us learning to submit to a power greater than ourselves. After so many years together, the pursuit is still active, keeping romance interesting. It is an inspired relationship.

Courtship with the Word of God is much the same. The Word of God came by way of inspiration and is understood by inspiration. We cannot mine its depths by sheer cunning any more than I could know my wife by reading a book about her. Surrender is necessary for true intimacy. And once intimacy and inspiration meet and agree, paradise is come again.

seasoned in the presence of majesty

This bunch was not the cream of Galilean society. Some of the 12 apostles were fishermen. Some were simple tradesmen. One was a tax collector. Scripture does not give us all the details. The details, as interesting as they might be, are beside the point. Just by the nature of the times, it is likely that while some were educated, some were not. The point is Jesus chose who he chose by an altogether different rule. He was making his own point, a higher one.

God hath chosen the foolish things of the world to confound
the wise; and God hath chosen the weak things of the world
to confound the things which are mighty.

1 CORINTHIANS 1:27 KJV

It is doubtful that an executive today would choose as Jesus chose—the simple, the ordinary, men who may have gone unnoticed by history at all had it not been for him.

This only makes the story that much better. It adds possibility to the mix.

Everything Jesus did had meaning. Since we have no permanent record of him writing anything down, I suppose it had to. The way Jesus chose the 12 preaches God's election. And in spite of the education they did or didn't have, it turns out that they were highly susceptible to inspiration. By the standards of apprenticeship, the three years they spent with Jesus was rather brief, but it was sufficient. John, the poet-prophet, writes:

> In the beginning was the Word, and the Word was with God, and the Word was God. He was with God in the beginning. Through him all things were made; without him nothing was made that has been made. In him was life, and that life was the light of men. The light shines in the darkness, but the darkness has not understood it.
>
> —JOHN 1:1-5

On your best day, you don't just sit down and write such words. This is the extraordinary awakened in the blood. This is deep resonance, the voice of our origins, the stir of deep memory, the fruit of an inspired life, of one who loves his master more than himself. The writer, *John, was seasoned in the presence of majesty. John, whose surrender grew bigger than himself and was as absolute as it was beautiful. John, who craved the company of his master, who never left his master's side. John, whose heart raced in happy riot at his master's return, the lovely John, who knew his master's voice even in a crowd, who knew the depths of his master's heart like none of the others. John, who laid his head on his master's breast at eventide, who cared little what others thought. John, who was not afraid to watch his master die, indeed, who understood the death, what it meant. John, who took his Lord's mother into his home as his own. John, who gave us the lyric "God is love,"*[4] *who in his old age was given the gift of revelation, the full contents of his master's heart unfolded to him. John, whose death could not be accounted for. John, who lived at capacity, who came at life with a full heart. John, for whom worship was a way of life. Beautiful, dedicated, intensely charming John.*

These 12 men were changed by spending time with the master, learning his voice, watching his movements, being confused by him, overturned and inwardly vexed by him, allowing love to meddle with them, to break their hearts so thoroughly, to have their feet washed so sweetly, hardly leaving his side for three years. Judas Iscariot was the exception. Misled, misbelieving, misguided Judas, our best proof that love is not a negotiation nor is our life in God. We know how he chose. (By the way, the name "Judas" means *praise*.)[5]

Christ made poets and wise men from ordinary humanity. The unimaginable was aroused in each of them and gave them words. Each began to live according to his origin, to a deeper nature awakened by Christ. Christ washed them clean of any other option.

The same was true of Saul of Tarsus, an educated young man, zealous and confident. Love washed him of his old life, of his old identity, even his name, and entrusted his words to him. First Corinthians 13, by any literary standard, is one of the finest works of lyricism ever written. Love has no choice but to sound the way it does, to speak in beauty and mystery. Love is inspired and has no choice but to inspire.

When you approach Scripture with awe, with a kind of trembling, only then will understanding come, saturating your heart with divine meaning. I am amused at the lengths we go to break it down, to decipher it, to sift it of meaning, and spit out the seeds. Such efforts reap small fruit. It is also a good indicator of how we love. Is my surrender alive and active like the word inside me? Or must I be in control?

We should take care to approach Scripture as a lover approaches his beloved, and with the faith that all I need is revealed and translated in some part of me God has reserved for himself. You might just think you are listening to music.

The devoted life is the inspired life. It is life at its most genuine, life as it was meant to be lived, life according to our original blueprint drafted by the hand of sovereignty. The devoted life, this authentic Christianity, this most genuine humanity enjoys the full consent and validation of heaven, and all the agreements of God, and all the benefits that accompany it. I have understanding, which is better than information. I have true wisdom, which is better than knowledge. I have peace, which is better than the mere absence of struggle. I have love, which is above all things.

• • • • • • • • • prayer of the inspired • • • • • • • • •

Oh, that I may come at life with a full heart, with all my senses flush immediate. Lord, give me a deeper, warmer sense of life around me that I may detect and seek out the lonely, the uninspired, the lost and forgotten, that I may stop and engage with life as it gathers itself to me, life as complicated, as confused, and as desperate as my own. That I may offer myself in fellowship. That I might offer a word of comfort. Give me eyes to see the beauty in all things you have made, great and small. I want to live as you intended me to live. Like Solomon, I do not ask for riches. I do not ask for peaceful borders or for security. I ask only for an understanding heart, a heart not afraid to engage in the moment, in the necessary moment, a heart that can recognize when that moment is come. I ask for a mind that submits to the dominion you have established within me, a mind that does not question the mystery of you but celebrates it. I long to awaken from this slumber that I might no longer dream of life but may begin to live it.

In Christ, this deep drink of life. Amen.

May Christ be the only distance between you
and an unimaginable life.

the incredible journey

A good play needs no epilogue.

WILLIAM SHAKESPEARE
AS YOU LIKE IT

DURING THOSE YEARS THEY WERE WITH US, I traveled a good bit. Whenever the conditions were right, my wife and sons traveled with me. Though we tried a few times, kenneling the dogs seemed too much to ask of them. The fuss wasn't worth it. So as a rule, a friend of ours stayed at our house to watch over the animals. Her name is Becky. She loved the dogs, and they were crazy about her. Salem had this thing for her that resembled his thing with Benita, which included mild flirtation. Actually, quite a bit of mild flirtation.

The dogs got accustomed to the routine: Becky in, the rest of us out. She was like family, and the dogs respected her authority in our absence. But with us away they couldn't resist the temptation to press limits they might not press when we were home.

Salem had a way with the front gate. It was his toy. We no longer live in the same house, but I imagine to this day there are marks on the gate that say "David 2, Salem 5." It was a game he liked. One he was good at. He always found a way out when he wanted one, when desperate enough, and when we weren't looking. We were always a bit dumbfounded by his ingenuity.

With Salem's talent for exit strategies, with Oreo's evolved taste for mischief, and with Savannah suffering her usual lover's melancholy and general indifference to life now that I was out of town and not sure what to do with herself, the three of them just figured, *"Who's gonna know? Let's go…it's what we do."*

Once when we were out of town, all three of them worked their way out of the gate. I can see it now. The girls standing by watching Salem work his sleight of hand and then following right behind him. Out they went, probably observing a casual we-own-the-world kind of pace. Maybe a saunter. Or the lope. There was no need to bound.

When Becky discovered they were gone she panicked. For good reason. It is not easy to get them to come back once they are gone. Usually when they got bored with their explorations or if they got hungry enough, they came back, at the speed of unconcern.

Becky didn't call us immediately, thinking she might get the dogs back through the gate without sending signals of alarm. As she predicted and as it had happened before, Oreo and Salem came back, casual, indifferent, as full of bounce and sniff as ever. It was dusk, and for the two of them there was but fading interest in the world outside our gate. But there was no Savannah.

Becky waited. Hours went by. She called another friend of ours to help search for the missing dog. When Debi arrived, they separated and began to probe different neighborhoods and other areas looking for the fugitive dog. Some sense of dread came over them in time because of the busyness and energy of the outlying areas near our home. Our street was a quiet one, and yet not a quarter of a mile away were heavily trafficked roads and strip malls, the buzz and growl of higher life forms. This was suburban Atlanta. The pace was always accelerated. The roar and cough of the busy streets was unhealthy for dogs. Becky and Debi abandoned the search close to midnight and decided to call us.

A day went by and still no sign of Savannah. They made posters and put them in local grocery stores and gas stations. With all their efforts, there was no response.

Another day went by.

Finally, at a Kroger store some distance from our house, Debi was putting up another "Dalmatian Lost" sign when she saw a sign that read "Dalmatian Found." She called the number immediately. Getting directions, she found the young girl's house not far from the store. When she saw Savannah in the backyard, all the tension of the past few days was released, and not without a few sudden tears.

Debi understood my attachment to this dog. She could breathe again. When she recovered, she was amazed that Savannah had been found so far from home. She looked a bit weary, but she was all right. The dog—not Debi.

During this time in my life I had gotten into the habit of running. It kept me sane and healthy. Not having acquired a taste for treadmills or the uneven topography of neighborhood streets, I chose to run at a local high school track. There were three high schools close by, and though I tried each of them once or twice out of boredom, the track at Berkmar High School became my default track. The school was new, it was close to home, and the track had a freshly laid surface with a spongy top that made running easier.

Most of the time I had a companion with me when I went to the track: Savannah. It was usually late in the afternoon or early evening, so it was cool enough to leave her in the van with the windows open as I worked out. Or I would tie a lead to the fence. A few times she even ran with me. I used to speculate in a silly sort of way what she might be thinking as I circled around the same space again and again. *"What is this fool doing?"* Or maybe she didn't question it at all.

She is a beautiful dog, not easy to ignore, and one day two men who were also at the track tried (and failed) to get her attention. When I finished, one of them remarked how she would not take her eyes off me. They were amazed at her concentration and devotion. I just smiled.

To get to Berkmar, I always traveled the same path. It was just over a five-mile trip from our house to the school, passing two strip malls, a Lowe's Building Supply, three busy intersections, and a good stretch of four-lane road that led to the front of the school. I include all this detail because the girl who found Savannah found her at the track at Berkmar wandering around, as if looking for something…or someone.

When I heard this, amazement and shock ran together so swiftly it was difficult to know what to feel. It was a dangerous journey. This pilgrim dog had to cross heavily trafficked streets. And how she knew the way is still bewildering to me. We had always gone in the van.

The best answer I can offer is that her desire was desperate, that her sense of connection to me was severe and fearless. Once again desire outweighed consequence. It may be natural to the species, but that doesn't discount the beauty of it or diminish the lesson it teaches. By some inner compass, something old in the blood, driven by an intense devotion, she came looking for me. I was all that mattered to her.

Veterinarians to this day have no clue how this homing instinct works. From studies made, it is clear that neither scent nor vision is involved.[1] I can only suggest something greater and more powerful than instinct, something deeper and wider than our current science has scope to understand. Who knows when or how it started, or when it grew to such dimensions as it did within her?

There is an incredible journey within each of us, a homing instinct that will turn over a whole world just to be near him we call master. It knows no impediment. It respects no distances and fears nothing because love knows no fear. It takes the risks demanded of it and thinks little of the cost. It has only one speed, one true master, and it doesn't suffer half measures.

There is a pilgrim and a pilgrimage in each of us. If speech could be ascribed to this condition of the heart, it might sound like this:

> How lovely is your dwelling place, O Lord Almighty!
> My soul yearns, even faints, for the courts of the Lord;
> my heart and my flesh cry out for the living God.
> Even the sparrow has found a home, and the swallow a
>   nest for herself, where she may have her young—a
>   place near your altar, O Lord Almighty, my King and
>   my God.
> Blessed are those who dwell in your house; they are ever
>   praising you. Selah.
> Blessed are those whose strength is in you, who have set
>   their hearts on pilgrimage.
> As they pass through the Valley of Baca [weeping], they
>   make it a place of springs; the autumn rains also cover
>   it with pools.
> They go from strength to strength, till each appears before
>   God in Zion.
> Hear my prayer, O Lord God Almighty; listen to me, O
>   God of Jacob. Selah.

Look upon our shield, O God; look with favor on your
    anointed one.
Better is one day in your courts than a thousand elsewhere;
I would rather be a doorkeeper in the house of my God
    than dwell in the tents of the wicked.   ⁕
For the LORD God is a sun and shield; the LORD bestows
    favor and honor;
no good thing does he withhold from those whose walk is
    blameless.
O LORD Almighty, blessed is the man who trusts in you.

—PSALM 84:1-12

absolution and a final bit of dogma

Compared to the mischief, the intrigues, the warm native devotion of the other two dogs, I thought Savannah was so immersed, so smitten to the point of ruin, so consumed with love that she might not possess the intelligence or the savvy the others had. I always thought her warm, but dumb.

Was I ever wrong!

It took severe love to brave those streets, the howling cars, the strangeness of foreign neighborhoods. But her devotion didn't give her much choice. My perception of her was totally undone. It changed me. I became more attached. The connection between the dog and me took a long step forward, and I wasn't sure that was even possible. But it was. What certainties there were became even more certain.

This same sweet dynamic exists between God and me. Or I would like to think so. Love is boundless. It knows no bottom. It gives all it has. Its possession is complete, absolute.

I agree with Shakespeare about an epilogue. A good play needs no excuse. A final word is probably unnecessary. Hopefully the point has long been made, and in spite of my fumbling, the metaphor long exhausted. But more than all the stories that accumulated around my dogs, this one story about Savannah taught me the most. Sure, God made man in his image, but Savannah's journey comes right on our heels. It is to be admired. Our resolve should be so immutable, so well defined.

Divinity is not aloof from nature. God put a share of himself in all creatures. Savannah taught me that love knows no fences, that the highest walls cannot keep love out or keep it in.

To this day, I miss that dog. I miss all of them.

In the end, like the other two, we had to euthanize Savannah. Again I had to make an awful decision. I had to face the same resistance within me I had known a couple of years earlier. And having experienced it once didn't make it any easier. The investments we had made were deep. Savannah was 15. She had lived a full life, and I suspect her devotion had everything to do with it. Or it is nice to believe that. Her love was a medicine we all benefited by.

At the end, in her own way, she let me know it was time, that she had done all she could, that she had given me her best, that she would let me go and trust me to the great mystery of life beyond her. Under another cloudless sky, I walked out into the parking lot of the animal hospital and wept with a full heart.

It has been said that dogs have no souls. Maybe it does or doesn't matter. It's not an argument I care to make. But my question would be how could any creature love so purely without one? It is difficult to imagine a heaven without their kind.

I have often thought what it might be like when my own time comes, when my footfalls are heard at the gates of heaven. What might my welcome be? Will I be greeted with a blast of trumpets or the song of angels? Either one would be nice. But I had another thought.

No, give me bustle. Give me the comic riot. Greet me with pant and clamor. Greet me with the wild exultant joy of dog love: perfect, complete, and above all true, love that seems at home wherever it is but especially here. Give me three wet black noses pressing eager and impatiently through the gates. Give me the old music, the whine and the howl, the high lonesome cry of jubilee. Sweetness and homecoming overflowing all our cups, as if I am given complete absolution for my crime against them, a full and undoubted pardon. Truth is, I don't think they held anything against me at all. They never could. And thereby hangs a tale.

notes

chapter 1: so inevitably dog

1. 1 John 4:8,16.

chapter 2: presence is everything

1. "Love does not delight in evil but rejoices with the truth" (1 Corinthians 13:4).

2. "Alpha": socially dominant, especially in a group of animals; first position.

3. 1 Thessalonians 5:17.

4. From *Fioretti di San Francesco d'Assisi* [Little Flowers of Francis of Assisi]. Grand Rapids: Christian Classics/Ethereal Library, www.ccel.org.

5. 1 Kings 8:10-11.

chapter 3: it's almost like being in love

1. "God is love": 1 John 4:8,16; "God is light": 1 John 1:5.

2. "Above all, my brothers, do not swear—not by heaven or by earth or by anything else. Let your 'Yes' be yes, and your 'No,' no, or you will be condemned" (James 5:12).

3. Most reliable sources on the life of Mary Queen of Scots do not name the dog (Antonia Fraser, Alison Weir, John Guy, David Willson, to name a few). At least one Internet source says the dog's name was Geddon. I hope they are right. Such a wonderful creature deserves a name. Sources say the dog was a Maltese or Skye Terrier. It was a small, devoted dog. For me, that is the strongest compliment to the creature. Anything else is wide of the point.

4. Roger Caras, *A Dog Is Listening* (New York: Simon and Schuster, 1992), p. 52.

5. "These men are not drunk, as you suppose. It's only nine in the morning! No, this is what was spoken by the prophet Joel: 'In the last days, God says, I will pour out my Spirit on all people. Your sons and daughters will prophesy, your young men will see visions, your old men will dream dreams. Even on my servants, both men and women, I will pour out my Spirit in those days, and they will prophesy' " (Acts 2:15-18).

6. "When they came to Jesus, they found the man from whom the demons had gone out, sitting at Jesus' feet, dressed and in his right mind; and they were afraid" (Luke 8:35).

7. See 2 Samuel 6:14-22.

chapter 4: saint bernard

1. Thomas Merton, *The Last of the Fathers* (Trappist, KY: The Abbey of Gethsemani, 1954).

2. Bernard of Menthon (932–1008), a Benedictine monk who dedicated his life to the salvation of others.

3. Pope Pius XII, *Encyclical Letter on the Occasion of the Eighth Centenary of the Death of Saint Bernard,* May 4, 1953.

4. William Shakespeare, *Romeo and Juliet*, Act II, scene 1.

5. Matthew 11:12.

6. The Oxford English Dictionary (Oxford, England: Oxford University Press, 2009), s.v. "desperate."

chapter 5: oh, how the world doth wag

1. "The man of the tombs," see Mark 5:15; Luke 8:35.

2. Bernard of Clairvaux, in his own way, was much like Elijah. A different time, a different commission from God perhaps, but just as severe a dedication to the master. In circa 1130 Bernard confronted William X, Duke of Aquitaine, father of Eleanor of Aquitaine, and told him that God disapproved of him because he supported the antipope Anacletus II against Pope Innocent II. William was incredibly powerful. He had more lands and wielded more power than the king of France. Indeed, William of Aquitaine possessed the largest domains in northwest Europe. Anacletus excommunicated Bernard. One day while Bernard was preaching at a church, William burst in armed and prepared to kill Bernard mid-sermon. Bernard held up the elements of the Eucharist (the bread and wine) and William immediately had some kind of a fit. He fell to the ground and foamed at the mouth. Wisely he decided that perhaps God was behind Bernard after all.

3. 1 Kings 19:1-2.

4. 1 Kings 19:3.

5. 1 Kings 19:10.

6. Matthew 17:1-3.

7. I particularly like the archaism of the word "loafe." The added "e" has the appearance of something old and forgotten, something devalued, something to be refound.

8. Thomas Merton, Thoughts in Solitude (New York: Noonday Press, 1958).

chapter 6: if i love you, who cares what time it is?

1. Homer, The Odyssey, Book 17.

2. Genesis 2:23.

3. Luke 21:4; see also Mark 12:44.

4. Job 13:15 NKJV.

5. See 1 John 3:2-3.

6. 1 Kings 18:17. I have paraphrased this verse. The verse has Ahab saying to Elijah, "Is that you, you troubler of Israel?"

7. 2 Kings 9:32-36.

8. I know the word "prophetic" is suspect to some. Indeed, it has seen some abuse. That doesn't weaken or alter its true meaning, power, or its employment by God. I use it in the sense of the part of God he actively shares with us, at times independently of us. We need not fear the word "prophetic" any more than we need to be afraid of God. As the Scriptures attest, "The testimony of Jesus is the spirit of prophecy" (Revelation 19:10).

9. Hebrews 4:12.

10. Jeremiah 31:34.

chapter 7: stick your head out the window if you don't believe me

1. Oxford English Dictionary, s.v. "contentment."

2. Matthew 28:20.

3. See Mark 5:2-15.

4. Genesis 1:26.

5. Hosea 1:2-3.

6. Psalm 19.

7. Genesis 1:2 KJV.

8. "Repent": "[GR *metanoia*] the act or process of changing one's mind" (OED). It also suggests that we "look again."

9. Ruth 1:16 KJV.

chapter 8: the joy of being who i am

1. Merton, Thomas. *New Seeds of Contemplation* (New York: New Directions Books, 1961), p. 35.

2. Ibid., p. 37.

3. Matthew 16:24; Mark 8:34.

4. Matthew 16:25.

5. Matthew 7:12.

6. Hebrews 12:2.

7. Hebrews 2:10.

8. Ludwig Mies van der Rohe (1886–1969).

9. Augustine of Hippo, *Confessions*. Book VI. New York: Spiritual Classics, 1977.

10. "If we confess our sins, he is faithful and just to forgive us our sins, and to cleanse us from all unrighteousness" (1 John 1:9 KJV).

11. Oxford English Dictionary, s.v. "righteous."

12. Nehemiah 8:10.

13. Alighieri, "Paradiso," Canto XXXIII.

14. "Genius": "[root Latin], *to beget*. Greek, *to be born, come into being*" (OED). Here too it implies origins.

chapter 9: if only i could love like that

1. John Keats, letter to Fanny Brawne, 1820.

2. Genesis 2:18.

3. John 15:17.

4. Matthew 21:12; Mark 11:15; John 2:15.

5. Matthew 21:12; John 11:35; Luke 7:38.

6. Matthew 12:30.

chapter 10: and finally, it was my dogs who taught me to stop and smell, well, everything

1. "Inspired": "*God-breathed* (L. *inspirare* 'to blow or breathe into,' f.)." The Latin "*spiro*" means "to breathe, blow; to exhale; to give off odor of, smell of; to aspire to" [New College Latin & English Dictionary (New York: Bantam, 1995), s.v. "inspired."

2. Ecclesiastes 1:12 KJV.

3. Deuteronomy 29:29.

4. 1 John 4:8,16.

5. Warren Wiersbe, *Bible Exposition Commentary* (Colorado Springs: Victor Books (David C. Cook), 2001), s.v. "Genesis 29:35." "She conceived again, and when she gave birth to a son she said, 'This time I will praise the Lord.' So she named him Judah" (Genesis 29:35).

Epilogue: the incredible journey

1. Jeffrey Masson, *Dogs Never Lie About Love* (New York: Crown Publishing, 1997), p. 59.

Bibliography

Alighieri, Dante. *Vita Nuova,* trans. Mark Musa. Oxford: Oxford University Press, 1992.

_____. *The Divine Comedy: Paradiso,* trans. A.S. Kline. Oxford: Oxford University Press, 2001.

Augustine of Hippo. *Confessions,* Book VI. New York: Spiritual Classics, 1977.

Baudelaire, Charles. "The Faithful Dog," *Paris Spleen.* New York: New Direction, 1970.

Bernard of Clairvaux. *On Loving God.* Grand Rapids, MI: Christian Classics Ethereal Library, www.ccel.org.

_____. *Sermons on the Song of Songs (Canticle of Canticles).* Paths of Love, www.pathsoflove.com/bernard/song of songs/contents.html.

Brother Lawrence. *The Practice of the Presence of God.* Grand Rapids, MI: Christian Classics Ethereal Library, www.ccel.org.

Caras, Roger A. *A Dog Is Listening.* New York: Simon and Schuster, 1992.

Eldredge, John. *Wild at Heart.* Nashville: Thomas Nelson, 2001.

Francis of Assisi. *Fioretta di San Francesco d'Assissi* [Little Flowers of Francis of Assissi]. Grand Rapids: Christian Classics Ethereal Library, www.ccel.org.

Garber, Marjorie. *Dog Love.* New York: Simon and Schuster, 1996.

Gibran, Kahlil. *The Prophet.* New York: Knopf, 1923.

_____. *Jesus the Son of Man.* New York: Knopf, 1928.

Grenier, Roger. *The Difficulty of Being a Dog.* Chicago: University of Chicago, 2000.

Grogan, John. *Marley & Me.* New York: Harper Collins, 2005.

Guyon, Jeanne. *Union with God.* Auburn, ME: Christian Books, 1981.

_____. *Experiencing the Depths of Jesus Christ.* Auburn, ME: Christian Books, 1975.

Houston, Jeanne. *Mystical Dogs.* New York: Oakland, 2002.

Hummel, Charles. *The Tyranny of the Urgent.* Westmont, IL: InterVarsity Press, 1967.

John of the Cross. *Ascent of Mount Carmel,* 1582-1588, trans. Alison Peers. Ligouri: Triumph Books, 1991.

_____. *Living Flame of Love,* 1585-1587, trans. Alison Peers. Ligouri: Triumph Books, 1991.

Levi, Allen. "I'd rather be a dog than a dude like you," *Talking with Tyler* (musical recording). allenlevi.com.

London, Jack. *White Fang.* London: Penguin Books, 2008.

Maeterlinck, Maurice. *Our Friend the Dog.* New York: Dodd, Mead, & Co., 1913.

Mann, Thomas. *Death in Venice*. New York: Random House, 1954.

Masson, Jeffrey Moussaieff. *Dogs Never Lie About Love*. New York: Crown Publishers, Inc., 1997.

Merton, Thomas. *New Seeds of Contemplation*. New York: New Directions Books, 1961.

_____. *Thoughts in Solitude*. New York: Farrar, Straus and Giroux, 1958.

_____. *The Last of the Fathers*. New York: Harcourt, Brace, Jovanovich, 1954.

Nietzche, Freidrich. *Thus Spake Zarathustra*. New York: Modern Library, 1995.

Nurbakhsh, Javad. *Dogs from a Sufi Point of View*. London: Khaniqahi-Nimatullahi, 1989.

Oxford English Dictionary. Oxford, England: Oxford University Press, 2009.

Pope Pius XII. *Encyclical Letter on the Occasion of the Eighth Centenary of the Death of Saint Bernard*. Given at Rome in St. Peter's, Feast of Pentecost, May 24, 1953, the fifteenth of our pontificate.

Shakespeare, William. *The Complete Works*. New York: Harcourt, Brace, and World, 1952.

Teems, David. *To Love Is Christ*. Nashville: Thomas Nelson Publishers, 2005.

Weir, Alison. *Mary, Queen of Scots, and the Murder of Lord Darnley*. New York: Ballantine, 2003.

Wolfe, Thomas. *Look Homeward, Angel*. New York: Scribners, 1929.

David Teems grew up in Atlanta, Georgia. His father was a worship leader in the church he grew up in, as was his father before him. But it was David's paternal grandmother who taught him the joy of words, the constructions, the magic they can make. She was the first to put an instrument in his hands (a guitar) at the age of seven.

David graduated from Georgia State University with a bachelor's degree in psychology. Pursuing a master's in counseling, he attended GSU. But following an altogether different passion, he abandoned the academic life and pursued music.

He married his wife, Benita, in a little ceremony presided over by Mylon LeFevre in 1984. David and Benita have two sons, Adam and Shad. Adam and his wife, Katie, have three children: Julian, Evie, and Audrey Gray. Shad will receive a BA later this year at a Tennessee university.

David has recorded seven albums and continues to perform often. But after God and Benita, writing is his first love. He will tell you his higher passions are literary (as well as some of his lower ones). His first book, *To Love Is Christ*, a devotional on love, was released in 2005. He is currently working on the book *Majestie: The King Behind the King James Bible*. His next book, *The Poet and the Morning Star*, focuses on the lives and work of John Wycliffe and William Tyndale.

For more information go to www.davidteems.com.